More Praise for *Two Birds in a Tree*

"Through an illuminating journey into ancient Indian wisdom, *Two Birds* describes a new type of leadership that can help us manage our businesses successfully and sustainably, rather than at the expense of the planet and people. It beautifully shows that the true sustainability of humanity is actually a matter of the heart and mind, compelling us to act consciously for the future rather than continuing to ignore today's realities."

—**Jochen Zeitz, Director, Kering; former Chairman and CEO, Puma; and cofounder of The B Team**

"*Two Birds* provides unique insight about the balance needed between our roles in meeting the financial goals of our business and in improving society. The reader can quickly identify with each bird and the branches we all navigate in our career and personal lives to enable continuous learning and adapting."

—**Kevin Kramer, President of Wiring Division and Vice President, Stoneridge, Inc.**

"Ram Nidumolu has done a beautiful service by reintroducing us to the ancient wisdom of the Upanishads. Far from being out of date, this wisdom is a contemporary, brilliant lamp that both exposes our current destructive ways and illuminates the way out of this perilous time. For those who yearn to offer meaningful leadership in service to this time, this book offers clear guidance."

—**Margaret J. Wheatley, author of *Leadership and the New Science* and *So Far from Home***

"A brilliant and inspirational look at how business—which today controls global economics and politics—can fix the messes it created. *Two Birds* encourages those responsible, now and in the future, to take the reins of leadership and truly lead."

—**John Perkins, author of *Confessions of an Economic Hit Man***

"Those who read Ram Nidumolu's remarkable book on the future of leadership will find a deep well of inspiration and wisdom. Both are things they desperately need at a time when so many of them are being forced to draw on their deepest selves to provide their people with purpose and a sense of direction."

—**John Elkington, cofounder of Environmental Data Services, SustainAbility and Volans Ventures and author of *The Zeronauts***

"Nidumolu's use of the Upanishads weaves an ancient story about Being that is still deeply relevant today but has been hidden by our Western ways of thinking. Being must be reawakened if we are to find our way out of the havoc our thinking has produced."

—**John Ehrenfeld, former Director, MIT Program on Technology, Business, and Environment, and coauthor of *Flourishing***

"People forget facts and figures, but they remember good stories. It's no accident that the world's great spiritual leaders all teach by storytelling. Great business leaders know this too. Ram Nidumolu is a master storyteller. Read him and reap—great results!"

—BJ Gallagher, coauthor of *A Peacock in the Land of Penguins*

"The most compelling executives today have mastered not only business strategy but the philosophical realms of social and environmental responsibility. *Two Birds in a Tree* cleverly explains how today's business leaders can leverage ancient Indian wisdom to achieve holistic corporate and personal success today."

—M. R. Rangaswami, founder of Corporate Eco Forum and Indiaspora

"The conversation about a new level of consciousness in business leadership is overdue. *Two Birds in a Tree* not only informs this important conversation. It inspires us with powerful stories rooted in ancient wisdom. I will share these beautiful allegories with colleagues and clients for years to come."

—Larry Dressler, author of *Consensus through Conversation* and *Standing in the Fire*

"A brilliant story-based approach to effective leadership, *Two Birds in a Tree* takes a very different path. Rather than offering the latest-and-greatest management theory or practice, it draws on insights from the world's oldest recorded wisdom, making it enormously relevant to today's business challenges."

—Dr. Chris Laszlo, coauthor of *Embedded Sustainability*

"*Two Birds* draws from the universal well of ancient wisdom and offers us stories and modern examples that literally change our minds about business. We imagine and live out of the idea of a separate self at our own peril and that of future generations. With this book, Dr. Nidumolu has provided the key that inspires and empowers us to change the mistaken idea of separation. It is a must-read for every person in an organizational leadership role."

—Yogacharya Ellen Grace O'Brian, Spiritual Director, Center for Spiritual Enlightenment

"*Two Birds in a Tree* is truly inspiring. The writing style is beautiful and authentic, attributes that are rare for a book intended for business. The balance between personal experiences, personal observations, stories of business leaders, and stories from Upanishads is just exquisite and quite a feat. This is a book I will read and reread, since a book like this is a highly personal journey."

—Mohan Sodhi, Professor of Operations Management, Cass Business School, London

TWO
BIRDS
IN A
TREE

TWO
BIRDS
IN A
TREE

Timeless Indian Wisdom
for Business Leaders

RAM NIDUMOLU

BK

Berrett–Koehler Publishers, Inc.
San Francisco
a BK Business book

Berrett-Koehler Publishers, Inc.
235 Montgomery Street, Suite 650
San Francisco, CA 94104-2916
Tel: (415) 288-0260 Fax: (415) 362-2512 www.bkconnection.com

Ordering Information
Quantity sales. Special discounts are available on quantity purchases by corporations, associations, and others. For details, contact the "Special Sales Department" at the Berrett-Koehler address above.
Individual sales. Berrett-Koehler publications are available through most bookstores. They can also be ordered directly from Berrett-Koehler: Tel: (800) 929-2929; Fax: (802) 864-7626; www.bkconnection.com
Orders for college textbook/course adoption use. Please contact Berrett-Koehler: Tel: (800) 929-2929; Fax: (802) 864-7626.
Orders by U.S. trade bookstores and wholesalers. Please contact Ingram Publisher Services: Tel: (800) 509-4887; Fax: (800) 838-1149; E-mail: customer.service@ingram publisherservices.com; or visit www.ingrampublisherservices.com/Ordering for details about electronic ordering.

Berrett-Koehler and the BK logo are registered trademarks of Berrett-Koehler Publishers, Inc.

Printed in the United States of America

Berrett-Koehler books are printed on long-lasting acid-free paper. When it is available, we choose paper that has been manufactured by environmentally responsible processes. These may include using trees grown in sustainable forests, incorporating recycled paper, minimizing chlorine in bleaching, or recycling the energy produced at the paper mill.

Library of Congress Cataloging-in-Publication Data
Nidumolu, Ram.
Two birds in a tree : timeless Indian wisdom for business leaders/ Ram Nidumolu, PhD.
—First edition.
   pages cm
Includes bibliographic references and index.
ISBN 978-1-60994-577-0 (pbk)
1. Management—Philosophy. 2. Leadership—Philosophy 3. Upanishads—Criticism, interpretation, etc. I. Title.
 HD31.N495 2013
 658-dc23   2013022539

FIRST EDITION
17 16 15 14 13   10 9 8 7 6 5 4 3 2 1

Cover designer: Steve Pisano
Composition: Beverly Butterfield, Girl of the West Productions
Copyeditor: PeopleSpeak

To

My father,
who led a life of integrity and inclusion

My mother,
who lives by faith and family

The Ātman,
which I have sought these many years

To Being's wide waters,
May the winds
Drive my life's actions.
ISHA UPANISHAD

CONTENTS

FOREWORD

In the wake of experiencing the magnificent Maha Kumbh Mela celebration on the Ganges River in the winter of 2013, Ram Nidumolu handed me the manuscript for this book and asked me to write the foreword. Initially, I was surprised. I'm a Caucasian from the United States. How can I comment on a business book imbued with timeless Indian wisdom?

But, then, I thought back to how miraculously connected I felt at the world's largest festival that occurs every dozen years in India (smaller Kumbh Melas happen there approximately every three years). Kumbh Mela is fascinating not just because of its heritage but also because of what it can represent for our future.

Harvard University's website notes that a temporary city is created every twelve years in Allahabad to house Kumbh Mela's many pilgrims. "This city is laid out on a grid, constructed and deconstructed within a matter of weeks; within the grid, multiple aspects of contemporary urbanism come to fruition, including spatial zoning, an electricity grid, food and water distribution, physical infrastructure construction, mass vaccinations, public gathering spaces, and nighttime social events."[1]

I was amazed by how a temporary city for 100 million people could be constructed and well managed over the course of the two-month religious pilgrimage. I asked one of the organizers of Kumbh Mela how this marvel occurred, and he simply said, "When you tap into the underlying spiritual needs of people—especially in an organizational context—be prepared to experience magic."

I have long been a believer in what I call *karmic capitalism*, the idea that eventually what goes around, comes around. This form of conscious capitalism recognizes the systemic effects—both organizationally and globally—of positive and negative intentions. What the world needs now are business leaders who recognize the ripple effect of their actions and decisions. Indian wisdom and philosophy are deeply rooted in the idea that we should evaluate the long-term, transformational effects of our influence rather than the short-term, transactional nature of how business usually operates.

One of the most valuable pieces of advice I ever received from a mentor was the suggestion that the more senior I was in an organization, the more I needed to think of myself as a role model. If you're a parent, you behave differently when you show up for your kids with the mind-set that you are a role model.

Your legacy is how you show up in life. Great leaders realize that they are the emotional thermostats and the oversized mirrors for those they lead. That's part of the reason I love this book so much. Ram has crafted a masterpiece not just for leading but also for living. If ever there was a book based on Gandhi's famous quote "Be the change you wish to see in the world," this is it.

One of my patron saints in business was Abraham Maslow, the humanist psychologist who created the iconic hierarchy of needs pyramid. Later in his life when he was studying the effect of positive psychology in companies, he coined the phrase *psycho-hygiene* to describe the intangible nature of what a healthy corporate culture provides its people. This is a book that will maximize the psychological health and hygiene of your organization and increase the probability of your peak performance. I hope you enjoy this book as much as I did!

CHIP CONLEY, founder of Joie de Vivre
Hotels and author of *Peak*

INTRODUCTION

Being Inspired to Lead

Being is One:
The wise say it
In many ways.
RIG VEDA

"This is business, not personal."

How many of us have heard this at work? It is as if we are expected to set aside our real being and put on our business persona when we enter through the corporate door. For that matter, how many of us ever talk of *being* in the workplace? Instead, almost all models of business leadership are typically about doing and having—that is, what should business leaders *do* in terms of actions and *have* in terms of capabilities to succeed? Yet these conventional models of leadership are failing us now as we careen from one global crisis to another.

This book is filled with more than forty stories meant to inspire business leaders to reimagine their role as human *beings* (rather than human *doings* or *havings*) in solving the global crises that business helped create. It includes stories from the wisdom of ancient India, personal experiences, and more than a score of examples of transformative business leaders. These timeless ideas are brought together through an overarching allegory of two birds in a tree that first appeared more than three thousand years ago in one of the world's oldest sacred texts.

A New Narrative

To be honest, this is not the kind of book that I thought I would write. While this book is descriptive and personal, my professional career has been largely prescriptive and impersonal. You see, I've spent the last thirty years immersed in business data and analysis—first as a student completing long years of doctoral studies in business, then as an assistant professor of business at research universities, next as an entrepreneur implementing business solutions based on customer and product data, and finally as a sustainability consultant and researcher helping senior business executives of Fortune 500 firms. I'm an analyst through and through, you may say.

But this is not a book for analysts. This is also not a book of business practices for solving the world's problems. The solutions are not so neat, simple, and universal that they can be listed as practices. Instead, this is a book that tries to inspire a new kind of leadership. I chose this approach for a simple reason: we are storytelling and story-seeking creatures who are moved by descriptions (not prescriptions) about the kind of person we want to be. This book aims to explore through inspiration rather than prescribe through practices.

We are at a turning point in our history, as our science and instincts tell us. What we do in the next twenty years in business will determine our future way of life, our children's heritage, and the fate of many species on Earth. It is hard to imagine that for our entire history until the 1800s, a person could expect to live for less than thirty years on average (while now that number is seventy). Indeed, for much of human history, our lives were "poor, nasty, brutish, and short," in the philosopher Hobbes's memorable phrase.

Capitalism and business (by which I mean modern industrial and services corporations) enabled the large-scale production of goods and services that lifted entire countries out of this misery in just two centuries. As a result, global per capita income increased tenfold between 1800 and today, with a hundredfold increase in America alone. All this progress was achieved despite the world's population increasing sevenfold, rising from 1 billion to 7 billion, in the same period. It is an economic achievement without parallel in the history of the world.

Yet this growth in human prosperity has come at a great cost to the larger context that is foundational to business, such as nature, humanity, and the credibility of the economic institutions of capitalism. Two-thirds of our water and land ecosystems (forests, wetlands, coral reefs, oceans, etc.) are now degraded significantly. We are at risk of a global warming of 4°C–6°C above preindustrial levels, largely because of industrial activity.[1] We are losing species at a hundred to a thousand times the rate of their natural loss. At this rate, we will kill off 30 percent of the world's species by 2050 and 50 percent by 2100.[2] We are triggering the sixth great extinction of species on Earth, called the Anthropocene since it is due to human industry.

Over twenty thousand children die every day from poverty, hunger, preventable diseases, and related causes.[3] The vast majority of the 100 million people who are expected to die by 2030 from pollution, hunger, disease, and natural disasters if the world does not act fast on climate change will be the world's poor.[4]

In America, only about 30 percent of employees feel engaged in their work.[5] This alienation has increased as the gains of business have largely accrued to those at the top. While the ratio of CEO pay to average employee pay in America was about 30:1 in 1980, it is now around 243:1.[6] The spate of corporate scandals in recent years has led to a crisis in the public's trust in the integrity of business leadership. In 2012, only 18 percent of the global public trusted business leaders to tell the truth.[7]

Yet these statistics have done little to fundamentally change business. Even worse, they seem to have numbed the public. Here's another statistic as proof: in a recent survey of twenty-two thousand people in twenty-two countries, the percentage of people who thought ecological problems were "very serious" had dipped to its lowest in twenty years.[8] We desperately need a different approach for making the case for change.

While people tune out as numbers foretell a dire future, narratives cling to the mind. We instinctively know what psychology has concluded: real change happens not through the practices of the reason-driven mind, which rationalizes what we have already decided, but through the emotion-driven mind, which is moved by the images that stories and other narratives evoke deeply.[9]

If the great English statesman Winston Churchill had said that he had nothing to offer but "more data analysis," instead of "blood, toil, tears, and sweat," as he roused his people to war, his message would have been much less compelling. This is why I will try to describe a new model of business leadership through stories.

The Fundamental Question

After three decades of observing, teaching, and participating in business and business leadership, I have come to the conclusion that something tremendously important has been missing all along. *It is the question of why business and business leadership exist at all.*

In truth, the buck stops with business leaders, such as corporate leaders and corporate investors. They are the ones who have to balance the interests of governments, the public, customers, other investors, and other stakeholders in business. If business is chiefly responsible for our current mess, then it makes sense that business should be chiefly responsible for fixing it.

When business leaders see business as disconnected from the world and pursue a purpose that is limited to themselves and their company, they are following a closed model of capitalism. They differentiate their company and themselves from others by asking, How can I do better than others within my closed system? How can I get a bigger share of a limited pie than others?

It is no wonder that the popular approaches are failing us because they do not focus on restoring the context so that business can operate well. We need a new purpose that puts the restoration of nature, our humanity, and institutional credibility at its core.

Business has tried to fix the symptoms without going to the root of the problem. It has done the minimum and given us corporate social responsibility initiatives that are peripheral to a company. Instead, what we need is a more inclusive approach that asks leaders to make the setting in which they and their companies operate central to their decision making.

In such an inclusive approach, while leaders recognize the importance of profits and growth, they don't see them as the primary goals. Instead, they see them as the outcomes of larger goals that preserve and renew the foundations of business.

Amid the pressures of everyday activities and the business demands of the short term, establishing the priority and resources to take care of the contextual foundations is hard unless there is a strong motivation to do so. For all these reasons, business leaders need to first get *inspired* before they are willing to act. But what's the key to inspiration's door?

Being: The Mother of All Concepts

My own experience has convinced me of the need for fundamental changes in the underlying beliefs that drive the mind-sets of business leaders. In turn, these beliefs are heavily influenced by a business leader's identity or sense of business self.

When our inner sense of our business self and our beliefs about business and its context change, then our behaviors, practices, and outcomes will follow. At first, this insight seems remarkably easy to implement—all we need to do to improve business is to improve the inner selves of its leaders. Of course, changing one's inner self is the ultimate quest and concern of the world's ancient religions and philosophers. Millennia have been devoted to this quest, yet the process of real inner change is rarely easy or clear.

When talking of identity or sense of self, we begin with the surface identities we assume in our personal and business lives. As we dig down, we realize that our sense of self is really much deeper than our surface identities, such as the organizational title given to us by our company. It is also much deeper than our attributes (such as our business skills, age, or gender) or even our definitions (such as our name).

As we continue this stripping away of identities, attributes, and definitions, we come to the question of who we really are at our core, behind the shifting qualities and limitations of our life. We arrive at the question, What is the essence of a human being? In doing so, we are revisiting an inquiry that is at least three thousand years old and gave rise to the world's first philosophical idea: the concept of a fundamental reality called Being that is beyond and prior to all attributes and limiting definitions.[10]

Put simply, Being is *the very essence of existence (to be) that is available to us at our core.* According to this view, all things in the world emerge from this reality, which is their fundamental essence. The philosopher-sages of the civilizations of Greece, India, China, and the Middle East twenty-five hundred to three thousand years ago were especially preoccupied with Being. It has been described in many ways (the One behind the many, Ultimate Reality, Truth, the Eternal, Godhead, and even God) and through many tongues (Brahman, Sat, Nirvāna, Tao, Sein, Ousia, Ontos, and others). It may be the mother of all concepts since it is about the very nature of existence itself.

Being and related concepts have transcended religious, spiritual, cultural, and philosophical boundaries over the past three thousand years and have become embedded in our ways of living and speaking today.[11] For example, there are eight forms related to the verb *to be* in English, more than those for any other verb. In truth, Being is relevant to anyone interested in what it means to be a human being.

The Upanishads

If the search for Being was the first philosophical quest, then ancient India was the place where this quest reached the peak of its early development. Insights on Being, our real identity or sense of self, and many other topics were explored in a series of texts, of which a group of philosophical books called the Upanishads is the most important. While hundreds of Upanishads have been written over time,[12] twelve to thirteen are considered the most important.

The Upanishads are also called Vedānta, or the end of the Veda. This is because they are the essence of the wisdom contained in the Vedas, the sacred works of ancient India that were foundational to Vedic religion and its later variation, Hinduism. However, because the Upanishads deal with Being, *they are meant to transcend Hinduism itself and be relevant to all religions and cultures.*

Many of the principal Upanishads were composed during 800–600 BCE, before the time of the Buddha. Although the authors of the Upanishads are unknown, they describe sages whose purpose was to educate disciples through instruction and their life's example. The Upanishads convey their wisdom through stories, assertions, imagery, exhortations, descriptions of procedures, and other forms of instruction. They were composed in Sanskrit, the language of the learned classes of ancient India and one of the oldest Indo-European languages.

While the imagery and language used in the Upanishads are often culturally grounded (and sometimes anachronistically male oriented), the underlying meaning is universal. For example, the Upanishads used the image of two birds in a tree to describe the inner struggle between selfish and selfless interests that we all face. I will use this metaphor and the journey of bringing these birds together as the book's overarching vision of how business leadership can restore the larger context of business while pursuing corporate-specific interests.

The stories in the Upanishads may sometimes appear simplistic and even repetitive, much like Aesop's Fables or other folk tales. But this very simplicity and repetition of truths are what lead to a deeper illumination. The core truth the stories convey is that Being is the foundational reality of this world and is accessible to everyone. Moreover, this realization is the best of all human knowledge.

While different ancient religions and cultures have resonated with the central concepts of the Upanishads,[13] for me, there is a personal reason. As a person of Indian origin, I have developed a particular fascination with and understanding of the Upanishads in the last twenty-five years. In the process, they have become "the consolation of my life, and will be the consolation of my death," as the German philosopher Schopenhauer wrote. My own experiences in applying the Upanishads have given me a direct perspective on leadership approaches. I will draw on them throughout this book as I outline the journey to Being-centered leadership.

Being-Centered Leadership

Being-centered leadership is the *effort to lead from a place of seeking to realize Being*. Because this realization is never complete, Being-centered business leadership is an ongoing effort to apply one's sense of Being to business life—it is a vision of leadership at its highest level.

A key part of Being-centered leadership is to realize that we are damaging ourselves when we damage the larger context that is foundational to business. Moreover, a sense of shared purpose in restoring these foundations is not at odds with individual purpose. It is central to its realization.

Given that Being has preoccupied millennia of religious thinkers, philosophers, and cultures, it is not too much to ask that it be included in business thinking and action too. It has been a central quest of our species, especially when we faced existential crises, and it is what helped us reconnect to our world.

As such, Being is the inspiration for making the contextual foundations of nature, humanity, and institutional credibility central to business leadership. With the help of the Upanishads, my own experience, and examples of many CEOs of our time, I hope to illustrate the importance of an awareness of Being for business leaders.

Who Should Read This Book?

While this book is about business leaders in corporations and investment firms, it is really for all people who are interested in playing a leadership role (regardless of their position in an organization) in enabling the better world that is the promise of real capitalism.

The purpose of this book is to inspire inner change in aspiring business leaders. This book is therefore about how to be an entrepreneur of the inner world in order to fundamentally transform the way business operates.[14] Since everyone has an interior, every person associated with business has the potential to be a business leader. More important than job title is the sense of curiosity, caring, aspiration, and search for meaning in the reader.

If this book is meant for every aspiring leader, then why focus on stories of CEOs? The first reason is pragmatic: more than anyone else, the CEO is the person most responsible for managing the relationship between the company, its stakeholders, and the world at large. As a result, CEOs have the most opportunity for integrative leadership and the most influence on a company's journey toward real capitalism. The second reason is vicarious: we are all curious about what it is like to be a CEO and to face the challenges that CEOs face. CEOs are the showbiz celebrities of the modern world where the main show in town is business.

The third reason is motivational: we repeatedly hear about CEOs behaving badly and losing the trust of society, but we hunger for stories of CEOs who can inspire us with their values, beliefs, and actions. And the final reason is exemplary: despite the difference in influence, CEOs have experiences that are relevant examples for our own settings since they deal with changes to an interior world where we are essentially similar. We are all human and subject to similar internal struggles.

How to Read This Book

Though we have much in common with one another, no two journeys are the same in the exploration of Being. Just as even a well-embellished road map does not reveal the specific distances, the pitfalls and shortcuts, and the stops and starts along the way, this book too may not give you all the details you may want. It is important to keep in mind that the goal is inspiration, not detailed practices.

I have provided a four-stage road map—the REAL road map—as a way to organize what can be something of a messy topic. But it is best to think of the book as a broad narrative that embellishes the road map, sometimes taking detours to see interesting wonders, often describing ancient and contemporary stories along the way, occasionally encountering strange sights that need another visit to understand, and frequently pointing out personal experiences that deepened my own journey.

A great deal of this cultural landscape may be new, as if the road map were now suddenly written in a strange language and marked with strange names, symbols, and other references that your cultural upbringing cannot interpret readily. You'll need to remind yourself that you don't have to understand every sign and conversation or pronounce every name well, that you are only passing through to get a feel for the place and region.

During this exploration, you may become impatient and want to be told what to do: Which specific road should I take and where should I turn and where should I stop for nourishment? I'm afraid I'll not have many of these answers because this is only a road map. You will have to create the guidebook yourself because this is your own unique journey, after all. Two helpful pointers are the "Tweets and Seeds" sections at the end of every chapter—the former lists the key conclusions in tweetable form (less than 140 characters each), while the latter provides food for deeper thinking. Together, they provide an easy way to grasp the many ideas in this book.

Despite this help, if the concept of Being remains relatively unfamiliar even at the end of this journey, you are in good company. Being has continued to remain elusive even after the best minds, storytellers, and sages in history have tried to explain it. This is because Being is (by definition) beyond the reach of our ordinary senses. Yet it is something we also grasp intuitively since it is the essence of our own beingness. *So near, yet so far—this is the irreducible mystery of Being.*

Why then should you even attempt this exploration, if all you have is a high-level road map with some interesting scribbles? For the same reason that hundreds of millions before you have: to understand themselves better, to know who they are and where they came from as they make this inner journey.

In exploring this oldest of questions there is the opportunity to change business, and through it, the world itself. In the poet T. S. Eliot's memorable phrase, there is the hope that "we shall not cease from exploration, and the end of all the exploring will be to arrive where we started and know the place for the first time."

This is the promise of Being-centered leadership.

TWEETS

- What business does in the next 20 years will determine our way of life, our children's heritage, and the fate of many species on Earth.

- We are well on our way to the 6th great extinction of species on Earth, called the Anthropocene since it will be due to human industry.

- Business needs a new purpose that puts a restored larger context at the center of its decision making.

- Being is the very essence of existence (*to be*) that is available to us at our core.

- Being-centered leadership is the effort to lead from a place of seeking to realize Being through business.

SEEDS

- To what extent do you think future technologies will address the problems we face today? Are all these crises really overblown?

- How much do the needs of the contextual foundations of business figure centrally in your own company's decision making?

- How important has your own identity or sense of self been in shaping your personal beliefs and behaviors? Which identities do you most relate to?

- How relevant do you think the ancient concept of Being is to today's world? How might you adapt it to a modern setting such as yours?

- What is the role of inspiration in encouraging changes in your behavior?

PART I

Being-Centered Leadership

We see great changes in this world.
Mountains falling down, . . .
The wind-ropes being cut,
The earth being submerged, and
The gods departing from their places.

MAITRĪ UPANISHAD

1

Being in Business

He who sees himself in all beings,
And all beings in his own self,
Loses all fear and embraces the world.
ISHA UPANISHAD

"There are two birds, two dear friends, who live in the very same tree." So say the Upanishads, ancient Indian philosophical texts about the nature of reality.[1] "The one lives in sorrow and anxiety and the other looks on in compassionate silence. But when the one sees the other in its power and glory, it is freed from its fears and pain." These two birds are symbolically perched at two different levels in the tree.[2]

The first bird, which lives in constant anxiety, is in the lower branches of the tree. Its view obstructed by the many branches of the surrounding trees, it hops around nervously, pecking at fruit both sweet and sour. So focused on eating fruit, it loses sight of the world around it and gets caught up in satisfying its immediate material desires. It is disconnected, in a way, from its environment and other beings and jumps from branch to branch, from one disappointment to another.

The second bird is perched atop the tree itself on its main trunk. From this highest perch, it has the broadest view of the tree and the lower bird. It can see vast expanses of earth stretching outward for miles and miles. It sees its feet attached to the tree, feels connected, and sees the lower bird moving frantically, following appetite after appetite, as it strips the tree bare of its fruit. The second bird does not eat fruit but simply watches, content to Be in its place at the top of the tree.

Like most images in the Upanishads, this one is an allegory for life. We can also look at it as an allegory for how we lead our lives in business and how business itself works. By *business*, I mean the modern industrial and services corporations where many of us in industrialized societies work. The first bird—the bird moving from appetite to appetite—is the individual ego. This is the self we often are at work: feeling fearful and anxious, acting protectively, viewing our life narrowly, and constantly comparing ourselves with others to create our sense of self. It is the business persona we have come to adopt—it is analytical and impatient and measures its successes largely in material gains with little consideration for how those gains may impact the world.

The second bird, free of fear and confident of the future, is the Being (Brahman) that is the foundational reality of the world.[3] It is described as a golden-hued bird that is also the universal self (Ātman), the authentic, unbounded, and everlasting self of all living beings. This fearless presence within us enables us to view our human condition with compassionate understanding and a larger perspective. This perspective is often missing in business.

Although the concept of Being is hard to define precisely, it broadly refers to our essential nature, or quality of existence, which we share with all other living beings, human or not. This shared commonality, or essence, gives living beings their name. Because of it, we call ourselves living *beings*; we are neither living *doings* nor living *havings*.

Today, much like the lower bird in the Upanishads, business seems to have lost its genuine sense of connection to humanity, nature, and its institutional credibility, which is the larger context within which it operates. It has lost its sense of Being. Many business leaders seem to have distanced themselves from the rest of the world, and the impact of business decisions on the world outside the company rarely appears to be a central factor.

Such a sense of separation is one major reason for the great ecological, humanitarian, and institutional crises that threaten our very existence and well-being—the growing threat of climate change, the ongoing destruction of ecosystems and biodiversity, the growing public concern with ethical breaches among many businesses, the spreading inequality between business executives and other people in society, the seeming disregard for societal well-being by financial institutions and other large corporations, and the increasing alienation of employees from their corporations. Business as usual that is based on separation from humanity, nature, institutional credibility, and ultimately Being engenders crises as usual.

How can we respond to these overwhelming crises that seem to be converging in ever-increasing fury? Human beings have a deep and shared connection with other humans, as well as with other living beings in nature and with the world itself. Being-centered leadership[4] is about anchoring in this foundational reality of shared connections. It is about freeing business to renew itself while simultaneously restoring balance to its shared connections to its larger context.

It is about how we can *be* as leaders to alleviate business's deep schism with humanity, nature, and its credibility with the public. Being-centered leadership is the effort to lead from a place of seeking to realize Being. In terms of our allegory, it is the great quest to realize the higher, golden-hued bird within us while engaging with the world through the lower bird that we embody. The end goal is business that is more holistic and sustainable in the long term because it continually nurtures the larger context in which it is deeply and existentially embedded.

The Axial Age and the Upanishads: Wisdom of the Sages

We can find inspiration for dealing with our multiple crises by considering the period 800–300 BCE, called the Axial Age.[5] The common emphasis of Axial Age philosophies was not so much on what you believed but on rediscovering the fundamental nature of the human being and who you were as a person. When this realization of our core nature occurred, changes in our beliefs, values, and behaviors followed naturally. The Axial Age is relevant for developing a new model of business leadership today in three ways:

- First, the changes and uncertainty about the future that we are seeing worldwide today are similar to those of Axial Age civilizations. Wars, migrations, natural calamities, and the disintegration of long-established empires and civilizations caused tremendous turmoil and societal strife.[6] It does not take much of a leap of imagination to see how the present age might be similar.
- Second, the business leaders of today exert an influence on society that is similar to that of the high priests of the Axial Age. Since the Industrial Revolution, the market economy has become central to everyday life, just as religion was central to the lives of Axial Age peoples. As a result, business leaders affect societal well-being like the priests did in the past.

    For example, business leaders have a major influence on the values and behavior of people, particularly with regard to work, consumption, and social status. In their impact on government policy and the officials who get appointed or elected, business leaders mirror the influence that the priests once had on rulers and royal policy. Through their understanding and control of the mechanisms of capitalism (the new "religion" of modern society), business leaders exert the kind of power that the priests exercised over religious practices.

- Third, the loss of trust in business leadership and corporations as institutions of capitalism today bears a remarkable similarity to the loss of public trust in the high priests of traditional religion in the Axial Age. Public skepticism sprung largely from the inability of these religions and their priests to explain the tremendous changes that were taking place and reassure the public about the future.

In the Maitrī Upanishad, the story is told of a king who turns to a wandering ascetic, rather than his priests, for counsel on how to cope with the changes. In describing these changes (summarized in exaggerated terms in the quote that begins part 1) and talking of his helplessness, the king laments, "I am like a frog that cannot escape from a waterless well. Only you can help me." Not only were the established religions and priests helpless in reassuring the people, they were themselves considered a chief cause of the disruption. The increasing demands of the priests for patronage imposed a large burden that led to public resentment and distrust.

The ways in which Axial Age civilizations responded to the changes that took place are hopeful signs for our modern-day Axial Age. Transformational ethical principles and practices developed in India, China, the Middle East, and Greece gave rise to the great religions of Judaism, Hinduism, Confucianism, Buddhism, Taoism, Jainism, and others. Even Christianity and Islam were later influenced by these practices.

While the particulars of each tradition were different, these religions had something of a shared commonality of wisdom—the connectedness of all and the rediscovery of the fundamental nature of Being.

The Principle of Correspondence

Let's begin with the word *Upanishad* itself. While its conventional meaning is that of sitting near a teacher for instruction, for the teachers and their students who learned an Upanishad, its real meaning was "hidden connection"—such as that between the two birds in the tree.[7] The individual who saw the hidden connections between the universal self and the individual self could also understand the correspondence between all beings in the world.

The Upanishads go even further: the persons who constantly saw this correspondence between themselves and other beings could *become* them. They could expand their consciousness and sense of self to *include* other beings they were connected to. In doing so, they developed a profound empathy with all beings in the world and with the world itself.[8] *This all-important principle of correspondence is central to the Upanishads.* To see a correspondence between two things was to recognize an essential similarity between them.

The principle of correspondence was not scientific and could be abused if it was applied too indiscriminately. However, it provided a metaphorical way of seeing the world that was closely aligned with how our minds function. As modern cognitive science has shown, the mind works primarily through a wide variety of conceptual *metaphors*—implicit comparisons between two seemingly dissimilar things that nevertheless have something in common—that are the building blocks of our abstract thinking.[9] We use metaphors to point out this commonality, or correspondence.

The Upanishads described this correspondence not just through metaphors (such as the two birds in a tree) but also through similes and other comparisons that made the meaning more vivid and memorable. The integrative vision of the Upanishads was of a world where a deeper structure and unity bound seemingly disparate and changeful things together.

Not only was this supposed to reflect reality, but it also had great pragmatic value. In the midst of uncertainty, one could take comfort in something that was stable and lasting. The value of this worldview is captured in one of my favorite verses in the Isha Upanishad (the most beautiful, simple, and lyrical of all the Upanishads): "He who sees himself in all beings, and all beings in his own self, loses all fear and embraces the world."

The Axial Age in India and elsewhere was indeed a period of tremendous uncertainty and change. Because the priests did not have satisfactory responses to the problems of the time, the Axial Age wisdom that developed in response was successful because it reminded people of their fundamental interconnectedness to one another, to nature, and to the world. Might a similar wisdom help business reconnect to the world—to Being—in this *Neoaxial* Age?

Being in Business

Many of the thousands of books on business leadership deal with issues that are relevant to the lower bird from the Upanishads: How do I work effectively? What qualities do I need to have to be successful? How do I get ahead in the world of business? Business leadership at this level is about doing and having, themes that are indeed important from this narrow viewpoint.

But if business leadership is about *being*, then an additional set of considerations becomes vitally important. These considerations have to deal with the commonality of existence that undergirds business, business leaders, and all other beings. A corporation, a start-up, a family-owned company, or any other business is then considered an integral part of an interconnected network of beings (whether individual or collective) that share the same foundational reality.

Moreover, the scope of business—such as business purpose and vision, stakeholders, success criteria, and management approaches—now becomes much broader to include these hidden connections (or externalities) of business to humanity, nature, and Being. Business leaders can no longer justify their actions solely in terms of the lower bird of material gain since Being-centered leadership requires a broader sense of collective and individual self that extends outward to humanity, nature, and ultimately Being.

Through the lens of Being-centered leadership, business is not just about the right to pursue material self-interest, such as material profits and growth, but also about recognizing and nurturing its connections to humanity and nature. The responsibilities toward them become an authentic part of such a sense of connection. Doing becomes guided by this broader vision and purpose. After all, if, under our law, corporations are treated as having many of the rights of individuals, can we not expect that they too have responsibilities for nurturing their connections beyond just profit? Shouldn't they be expected to have empathy, just as human beings do? These responsibilities extend even beyond the life of a business since its impacts survive its material existence.

The Upanishads tell us that these expectations are reasonable because of the principle of correspondence between human beings and corporations. All beings, whether individual or collective, are connected inextricably to one another because they are ultimately expressions of the foundational reality of Being.[10] When business leaders realize these hidden connections, they will *naturally* embody a genuine sense of the responsibilities that arise from these connections. In this way, business becomes more holistic through Being-centered leadership, thereby bridging its great schism with humanity, nature, and institutional credibility.

The story of the late Anita Roddick, founder and former CEO of the Body Shop, is an inspirational example of a Being-centered leader. Her connection to humanity was forged at the age of ten when she came across a book on the Holocaust.[11] What she saw "kick-started [her] into a sense of outrage and a sense of empathy for the human condition."[12]

Years later, Roddick set up a small cosmetics shop in England where she sold skin-care products to survive.[13] She was a big believer in the power of stories, and cosmetics allowed women to tell stories. She said, "[In] every group I have spent time with, women will always corral around a well and tell stories about the body, birth, marriage and death. Men only have conversations or memories about their first shave. But women will always use the body as a canvas, a playground. Even when they were taken to the gallows, women would always want to put some makeup on."[14]

The Body Shop became one of the earliest companies in the world to fight for protecting nature, but Roddick was not just about nature. She campaigned vigorously for tribes and indigenous populations in solving livelihood and human rights problems created by corporations, and she provided a sustainable livelihood for Amazonian Indian tribes by trading in brazil nuts, which produced an oil for moisturizing and conditioning. As she said, "For me, campaigning and good business is also about putting forward solutions, not just opposing destructive practices or human rights abuses."[15]

Other groups that Roddick worked with included indigenous tribes in India and Nepal, sesame seed farmers in Nicaragua, aloe vera growers in Guatemala, marula growers in Namibia, and the Ogoni people of Nigeria. She campaigned actively for Greenpeace and other activist organizations and led campaigns against the use of sweatshops by corporations, animal testing in cosmetics, unfair trade practices, domestic violence, and many other practices that demonstrated her passionate caring for humanity.[16]

Throughout all these causes, she built the Body Shop into a billion-dollar global corporation (or a multilocal business, as she called it)[17] with more than two thousand stores in fifty markets serving hundreds of millions of customers. She passed away in 2007 of a brain hemorrhage, leaving her wealth to charities and a company globally revered for its ethical principles.[18]

Roddick was a shining example of a Being-centered leader, connecting deeply and fearlessly to the larger context of business and fighting vigorously to preserve and renew it as an integral part of doing business. She was a true exemplar of the core principles of Being-centered leadership covered in this book:

- Seeing business as embedded in and deeply connected to a larger context of nature and humanity because of the relationship of these elements to Being (part 2)
- Recognizing that individual business purpose has to be aligned with a *shared* business purpose that preserves and renews the larger context of business (also part 2)
- Viewing the outer world of work as a projection of inner aspiration (part 3)
- Redefining business success as ensuring the long-term holistic health of all stakeholders (part 4)
- Having the courage to embody these principles in one's own life (part 5)

Being-Centered Leadership and Business Performance

Business leaders who are skeptical of the business worth of the principles of Being-centered leadership may well ask, Can such a Being-centered business also do well in terms of conventional measures of success, such as material profits and market value? If not, the case for such a business is a much harder sell to skeptical business leaders.

The outcome from a Being-centered business (which should more correctly be called a *beingness*) is a company that emphasizes ethically, environmentally, and socially sustainable business practices that also lead to financial success. All Being-centered businesses are sustainable businesses in terms of outcomes because they actively work to preserve and renew their larger context of nature, humanity, and institutional credibility.

So what is the evidence that sustainable businesses do better than other businesses, even when it comes to conventional measures of performance? In one of the most comprehensive analyses ever conducted, a team of researchers at Harvard Business School (HBS) compared ninety companies that voluntarily adopted environmentally and socially sustainable practices with ninety companies that did not.[19] The two samples were matched in terms of size, indus-try, and other variables, so that differences in performance would be most likely due to their stance on sustainability.

The HBS researchers found that the sustainable companies were more likely to be long-term oriented, had organized processes and procedures for engaging all their stakeholders, had incentives to compensate top executives on sustainability performance, and had boards that saw themselves as responsible for sustainability. On the whole, sustainable companies ran their businesses very differently from others.

The researchers tracked the performance of these two groups of companies over eighteen years, beginning in 1993. They found that sustainable companies outperformed the other companies signifi-cantly in market value as well as accounting measures such as return on assets and return on equity. For example, an investment of $1 in early 1993 in a portfolio of sustainable firms would have increased to $22.6 by the end of 2010, using market prices for the companies' shares. By contrast, a similar investment of $1 in the companies with no focus on sustainability would have grown only to $15.4.[20] This difference of 47 percent in market returns is large by any measure.

My own qualitative research on thirty Global 500 companies that are using sustainability to drive business innovation, which was pub-lished in the *Harvard Business Review* in 2009, came to similar con-clusions.[21] The message here is clear: regardless of how you measure performance, sustainable companies dramatically outperform other companies over the long term.[22]

All this evidence gives me confidence to conclude the follow-ing: Being-centered companies that deeply value their companies' connections to their larger context do better than those that don't, even on conventional measures of success. The challenge is that even when business leaders recognize the importance of the larger con-text, they often fail to make it central to their everyday decisions.

For many business leaders, short-term expediency overshadows the impact of their decisions on the larger context of business. This is because their recognition of the larger context is only skin deep. It has not penetrated their belief systems and personal and business identities so that they are willing to risk the consequences of making context-restoring decisions that don't pay off immediately.

The inspiring example of Anita Roddick shows how personal commitment and beliefs regarding the larger context of business (and the courage to act on them) are core ingredients of true leadership. The timeless wisdom of the Upanishads and the Axial Age show that such a commitment and belief system can result from the quest for Being, which can deeply reconnect business to its larger context.

If we are to solve the global crises that business helped create, it is time for business leaders to lead from the very human foundation that we call Being.

TWEETS

- *Being* refers to our essential nature, or quality of existence, which we share in common with all other living beings, human or not.

- Each of us comprises a lower bird of narrow ego and a higher bird of innate being, or universal self (Ātman), with a larger perspective.

- Being-centered leadership is our quest to become the higher bird while engaging with the world through the lower bird we embody.

- The word *Upanishad* means "hidden connection" between the world and us, a principle that applies to a person as well as a business.

- Axial Age wisdom can connect business to the world through Being-centered leadership.

SEEDS

- What do you think the "personal" responsibilities of corporations are? Where would you draw the line in comparing a business to a person?

- How can business leaders benefit from asking themselves who they truly are?

- What are the hidden connections of your business to the world that you or other business leaders often disregard?

- What do you think really keeps business leaders from including the larger context in their decisions (as Anita Roddick did), beyond the surface causes?

2

Being Connected

He who knows both doing and knowing,
Through doing overcomes death,
And through knowing attains immortality.
. . .
He who knows both the explicit and the tacit,
Through the explicit overcomes death,
And through the tacit attains immortality.
ISHA UPANISHAD

According to the Upanishads, the lower bird within us is concerned with the world of sense gratification—of pleasure and pain, happiness and sorrow. The behavior, capabilities, and motivations of this bird are relatively easy for us to track and understand because they are identified with our material body. The unity of matter, mind, life-breath, and intelligence comprises the material nature of the living person. This material self is something we are intimately familiar with; it gives us a point of view for everything we think and do.[1]

The concept of the higher bird in us, the universal or true self (Ātman), is the great and shining jewel of the Upanishads. The Ātman is the ground from which the material self is formed. It has been described as "The principle of man's life, the soul that pervades his being, his breath, his intellect, and transcends them. Ātman is what remains when everything that is not the [true] self is eliminated . . . there is an unborn and so immortal element in man, which is not to be confused with body, life, mind and intellect. . . . Our true self is a pure existence, self-aware, unconditioned by the forms of mind and intellect."[2]

Just as our material self is synonymous with our material being, the Ātman is the witness-consciousness within all living beings. It is the perfect, fearless, and innate being that is already present in every one of us, according to the Upanishads.

Being in the World

As a corporate sustainability professional, I frequently come across research and other evidence that shows the growing damage business is causing Earth and humanity. At these moments, I cannot help but fear that business has become so obsessed with profit and growth that it will not address the existential crises in time. The powerful and invisible hand of the market seems to have roughly brushed aside the caring palm of nature's enfolding presence. But once in a while, something breaks through to lift my hopes. It is the thought that something in us, a shared commonality of plight or some lost connection to what we are destroying, will eventually inspire collective action before it is too late.

I know where this sense that things will be all right comes from: it comes when I think of our unexhausted quest for Being that pervaded the philosophies of our ancient world. The ancients did not know much about management, science, and technology or anything at all about the great efficiencies of markets and self-interested corporations, but they were steeped in a sense of sacred connection to the world. Surely this subtle chord of connection lies somehow undiminished within us even as countless harsh symphonies of separation swept through our societies in the past millennia.[3]

When talking of Being and connection, I am reminded of an encounter involving Jeffrey Swartz when he was the COO of Timberland, an outdoor clothing and goods company. In 1989, Swartz had been invited to speak at a halfway house, where he encountered a struggling teenager who asked him what he did for a living. When Swartz responded that he was a COO, the teen said he did not understand what that meant, or what he did. Swartz then clarified that he was responsible for the global execution of strategy for a large company.

Then it was Swartz's turn to ask the teenager what he did. "I work at getting well" was the quiet answer. "That was an answer that sort of trumped mine," he later said. This simple and direct exchange between one human being and another was an epiphany for Swartz. A chance meeting with a troubled teen had reconnected Swartz not just to the teenager's humanity but to his own.[4]

Swartz returned to Timberland determined to make the company a force for human good. As CEO, he built a company that transformed its industry, generated $1.5 billion in annual revenues, and became a corporate icon for doing well while doing good. In 2011, Timberland was acquired by VF Corporation for $2 billion at a healthy $43 per share.[5]

In present-day business, examples like this are much more the exception than the rule. If business leaders recognize, trust, and act upon their latent connections to others as Jeffrey Swartz did, this doesn't necessarily have to be the case. Let's understand why Being is the source of these latent connections, through one of the most important stories from the Upanishads.

Being and the Universal Self

The Upanishads are filled with stories and instructions to realize Being, the foundational reality of the world. But how can one realize or even understand this reality, especially when it seems so much outside us? The Upanishads have a simple answer: *the universal self (Ātman) that is our essence is also Being itself.* To realize Being, all we need to do is to look inside because the universal subject immanent in us is also the universal object that transcends us.

In a story in the Chāndogya Upanishad, the sage Āruṇi explains to his son Śvetaketu how the Ātman is the ineffable essence of this world and all its beings. Through successive examples—of nectar that is gathered from different plants by bees and merged undifferentiated into honey, of rivers that merge into the ocean and lose their identity, of banyan trees that grow from tiny seeds that are their essence—Āruṇi explains that the Ātman is similarly the finest essence of every being in the world. Indeed, it is *the world's self.*

His final example drives this point home:

Āruṇi said, "My son, place a lump of salt in a jug of water and return tomorrow."

The next day, Āruṇi said, "My son, bring the salt that you placed in the water yesterday." But Śvetaketu could not find it, for it had completely dissolved in the water.

Āruṇi said, "Take a sip from this side, my son. Tell me how it tastes." "Salty," said Śvetaketu.

"Now take a sip from the middle. How does it taste?"

"Salty."

"Now take a sip from that side. How does it taste?"

"Salty," said Śvetaketu.

Āruṇi said, "In the same way as the salt pervaded the water, even though you do not directly see the Ātman, it is the subtle essence that pervades this whole world."

Lest we think that the Ātman is thus easily understood, the Kena Upanishad hastens to say that he who thinks he knows it does not really know, and he who thinks he does not know knows more than he believes. Indeed, the universal self cannot be grasped through our ordinary senses. Trying to understand the universal self through words is like trying to understand our own material self through someone else's description.

A secondhand understanding is vastly insufficient compared to our rich, subjective, inner experience of what it is like to have a material self. The presence of my material self allows me to engage with my body, other beings, and my surroundings in ways that are infinitely richer than any conceptual understanding of the material self and its relationship to the world.

In the same way, any conceptual secondhand understanding of the Ātman will be infinitely poorer than the subjective experience of it. This is why the Upanishads say that the senses, and even the mind, often turn away from the Ātman: because they treat it as merely an object when it is so much more.

Connection through Shared Humanity and Nature

If the ordinary senses cannot establish our connection between the material self and the universal self, then in what other ways can we do so? One way is to consider our hidden correspondence with other beings directly.[6] Not everyone necessarily has to have an aha moment like Jeffrey Swartz. Take a conversation that I had with Jochen Zeitz, the German-born, former CEO and chairman of Puma, a sporting goods and lifestyle company.

When I asked Zeitz about the role of Being in business, he said: "Everything is interconnected. The moment you take philosophy, psychology, religion, and business and look at the underlying commonality, that's when you start looking at business in a different way. It's important that you ultimately find your life through being, and not through having, once you cover your essential needs. But if you don't think you're covering your needs, 'having' becomes part of your being because you need to have in order to live."[7]

I asked Zeitz, "But how can this sense of Being be introduced in corporations, given that it is so unfamiliar a term in the language of business?" He said, "If you look at how much of our life we spend in business, do you want to wait until you're retired to say, 'Now I'm going to enjoy life?' I mean, shouldn't we ideally be in business as well as be working on what we think is very important in our life? It is about business helping give employees an identity, a culture—something they can utilize to be during their work. And it doesn't even have to say, 'It's about spirituality.' It's about being at work and being respected and being valued, having an ethical platform to work from in business, and having integrity in what you do—and that ultimately makes the work environment more fun too."[8]

And where does nature fit in all this? "Without nature, we cannot *be* in the long run," Zeitz said. "So not having nature healthy will ultimately have a very negative effect on everybody's sense of Being. It is critical that we recognize this fact. It is critical to the poor fishermen that no longer can fish to make a living because 50 percent of their fisheries are now depleted or to the poor in many areas of the world who are most affected by climate change. Nature has a significant impact on society, and there's just no choice but to value nature appropriately in order to find solutions."[9]

So, how do we go about creating this mind-set where Being and nature actually are valued? "It's not that there's one ultimate solution or answer," replied Zeitz. He went on to explain that just as we are all unique, we will need to find our own epiphany, our own reason, our own *connections*.[10]

But where do we go looking to realize these connections? Zeitz replied, "To me, psychology is something that helps us understand ourselves, something that helps me broaden my horizons into the areas that ultimately are affected by how I am doing things. But that's just my personal belief—that psychology and a better understanding of our conscious selves are helping us better understand the world around us and inside us. . . . It's kind of an unspoken language that is happening among us that has not been discovered yet. But it's subconsciously spoken in a way that connects us all. . . . It's more the connections that we have and that help us communicate without us being consciously aware of them."[11]

I asked, "But what role does nature play in this subconscious connection?" He answered, "Well, isn't that part of nature? We've sort of distanced ourselves from nature. Ultimately, we are part of nature. We just think we are above it, but it's quite the opposite. . . . We will never master nature. I think that's just a schizophrenic thought.

We need to work with rather than against nature because otherwise, nature will not take care of us."[12]

From the perspective of Being-centered leadership, every one of us is connected and has the potential to be a business leader because of the simple nature of our existence. Whether we are senior business executives such as Jeffrey Swartz and Jochen Zeitz or workers to whom no one reports, how we *choose to be* in our business lives affects the lives of the people with whom we interact. In turn, it influences the impact of the corporation itself on the broader world. In seeking an inner transformation to realize Being, there is the possibility of transforming the world itself because many good values, visions, and actions can flow from a centered, understanding, and open self.

From Why to How: The REAL Road Map

We have looked at the problems and crises resulting from the false separation between business and its larger context and the reasons why a turn toward Being-centered leadership is beneficial for the world and for business in the long term. But how do we make such drastic changes to the underlying motivators that ultimately drive us—that ultimately drive business? What are the steps that the lower bird in the tree of business life must take to realize the higher bird?

Imagine the lower bird perched on a side branch in a tree of life being besieged by a storm. The lower bird feels the cold, harsh winds flying all around it and looks up. It catches a glimpse of the higher bird sitting safely above the storm and *recognizes* something larger, something higher than itself. The recognition moves the lower bird to *experience* a connection to the higher bird more fully through its senses in ways that are special to its aspirations, strengths, and limitations.

This experience gives the lower bird a greater ability to feel the branch beneath its claws. With repeated practice, it is in a better position to *anchor* itself in this larger understanding, leading to a freedom from fear that is grounded in a steady vision of the higher bird. This safe anchoring enables actions that move the lower bird toward the higher bird, which inspires other birds through *leadership* by example.

Realizing that Being-centered leadership is also about *doing* is crucial because a sense of Being creates shared purpose and meaning to what leaders *do*. In essence, Being-centered leadership includes and guides lower levels of leadership that focus on *doing* and *having*.[13]

The journey of the lower bird to realize the higher bird is about a balance between pure doing and pure being, which Being-centered leadership achieves. Both are needed; pure being without doing is without outcomes, while pure doing without being is without higher purpose. Metaphorically, this imbalance occurs when the two birds are far apart in the business tree, while a fine balance occurs when they are together. The challenge is to bring the two birds together to achieve this balance.[14]

To maintain a balance between being and doing, Being-centered leaders also emphasize tacit as well as explicit knowledge (right brain and left brain) and value both inner work and external work (introspection and action). As the quote from the Isha Upanishad that begins this chapter tells us, all of them are valuable. A holistic view of leadership includes all these dimensions of knowledge and work to be effective.

Together, the two kinds of knowledge and the two kinds of work describe four broad stages of the journey or any segment of it. These stages and the sequence for undertaking them are the organizing principles or road map for this book, with a portion of the book dedicated to each stage of the journey. As with a road map, following a specific sequence of stages is recommended.

The road map itself is derived from the Isha Upanishad and my experience in applying the Upanishads to my personal and business life over the past twenty-five years. It was also developed from my consulting experience in implementing business change, as well as business research that describes how organizational and individual change takes place.

A version of the REAL road map was developed and tested in a global study I conducted of twenty-six pioneering companies that were global leaders in measuring, valuing, and managing their dependencies and impacts on nature. Sixty percent of these companies had more than $10 billion each in annual revenues. The results of the study strongly validated the four-stage road map that connected corporations to the nature-related aspect of their larger context.[15]

The REAL road map of the journey to Being-centered leadership consists of the following four stages in their recommended sequence:

1. *Recognize* a higher reality (*sat*), or the larger context of business, that is connected to the higher bird (Ātman), which is Being.
2. *Experience* this recognition through your consciousness (*chit*) in your own unique way so that the recognition is deepened and made more lasting.[16]
3. *Anchor* this experience in a mind-set that promotes joy (*ānanda*) so that it deepens your recognition and becomes the basis for your thoughts and actions.
4. *Lead by example* from this place of anchoring so that you become a Being-centered leader (*ātmana*) in thought, word, and deed.[17]

One reason I call this the REAL road map is that it begins with recognizing the *higher reality of business*, a term I will use interchangeably with the *larger context of business*. According to the Upanishads, that which is real (*sat*) is also true. For the Upanishadic sages, reality was truth, and that which was true was also real. But remember, this is only a road map, not the actual journey itself. You can follow the stages in any sequence, repeat one or more stages as needed, or follow some other combination that is tailored to your particular journey.

While the rest of this book is filled with stories that describe each stage in more detail, it is important to recognize that Being-centered leadership applies to large and small challenges, long and short time frames, and business and personal contexts. This is not surprising because the principle of correspondence sees a commonality between leadership over a lifetime, in response to a specific crisis, and in everyday moments in one's personal life. These everyday occasions for being in the moment provide inexhaustible grounds to practice the four stages.

Illustration: Being in the Moment

When I am feeling down, I often go for a walk along a high road by the beach near where I live. It is on walks like these that I feel closest to nature, that I feel a sense of stillness and peace, a slowing down, a being in the moment, even an occasional moment with Being. These walks are a microcosm of the four stages of Being-centered leadership that I have described above.

Since the principle of correspondence applies to things large and small, opportunities for Being-centered leadership are present in the microcosm of life's everyday challenges, as well as in the larger canvas of corporate leadership. In fact, how we respond to these microcosmic events is the woof and warp of the grander narrative we weave.

Consider the first stage, recognition. At rare times, more especially when I am without hope because of something that happened that day, an unvoiced and still presence seems like a dim light through a darkening sky. At extreme moments, I even fancy that it seems to say from within, *"Do not give up faith in me, for I am ever by your side."* Recognizing this evanescent thought or feeling, by becoming aware of and paying attention to it, is the first step of Being-centered leadership.

As I hold this thought's presence, there comes from within a familiar feeling, as though of a pooling inside, of depths that rapidly fill with another's empathy. *"I will grieve with you, even if there is no one else for you to grieve with."* It seems like the initiation of a cleansing of an internal mirror. It is a slow cleansing of all the negative thoughts accumulated over the day. The within holds the promise of filling with a quiet hope that all is already fine with me in this world, and this slowing down will be a testament to just being.

Then comes experience, especially when the decision to go for a walk is taken. At these moments following recognition, it seems that the ocean by my side, laughing with the flush of waves that lurch aside to avoid the diving pelicans, is filled with this recognition. Through waters bathed in the reflection of a setting sun—looking like pieces of mirrors gleaming in red on tossing foam—this silent thought moves swiftly through the squawking groups of gulls that catch my attention. It brings a moment's respite from the wearying self-recriminations.

Being here now is to hear the gulls as they wheel overhead and to see the setting sun as it splinters over the waters. *Now* is to see the ancient-seeming pelicans as they travel in great migrations over the waters or to see them as they rise and dive with fierce elegance on the trail of a shadow in the waters below.

Now is to see the dogs as they scramble joyfully on the beach below, to hear the murmur of casual voices on the path, and to see the road ahead as it hugs the coast as if to fulfill a silent compact of friendship. Most of all, it is to be alive, to be able to feel this presence again, and to feel this inner upswelling again.

The anchoring follows recognition and the deep experience of the moment. With the internal voice and the urge to slow down comes a sense of clearing, of the head and mind slowly being cleared of a large disquiet. A hundred hard thoughts that would otherwise have run deep down into an anxious valley now slow in their tracks.

The hardness in the mind and with the self, and especially with the self's sense of past failures, now turns slowly to soft acceptance. As I breathe deeply the evening air and as I feel my mind clear slowly from these deep anxieties, I can now see more clearly the waves and the pelicans, the seals and the surfers, and the paths and the people who walk and run and ride their bikes around me.

Now as I come to the end of my walk, the combination of recognition, experience, and anchoring provides a basis for my actions for at least the next few hours. To lead by example in these hours of opportunity is to rise above the crash of the immediate waves, even if it is for only a while. It reminds me of my brief glimpse of the pelicans that soared once again in splendor over wind-tossed waves after they had dived deep for their nourishment. They were here before humanity set foot on Earth and will hopefully be here after we are long gone.

These hours give me a window through which I see more clearly the real world beyond the distorted one that my fearful mind had created before my walk. But the window closes much too soon. My main challenge is to repeat these stages of Being-centered leadership often enough, for every disturbance or setback, that they become second (or rather, *first*) nature to me.

Let us now dare to look up from our rickety perch on the lower branch of a storm-battered business tree and begin the journey to the higher bird of leadership.

TWEETS

- The universal self (Ātman) is the shared essence of all beings and is Being itself, the foundational reality of the world.

- We can connect to the universal self (Ātman) or Being by valuing our connections to fellow human beings and with nature.

- Business work can be the equivalent of rituals for ancient civilizations—important for connecting us to humanity, nature, and Being.

- Being-centered leadership is about enabling business to think holistically about its relationship to the world.

- The REAL road map for being-centered leadership comprises the stages of recognition, experience, anchoring, and leadership by example.

SEEDS

- If Being is beyond the grasp of the ordinary senses, then how would you show it is still useful to a business that emphasizes tangible and measurable concepts?

- Have you had an eye-opening experience similar to Jeffrey Swartz's conversation with the teenager? What impact did it have on you?

- Is Jochen Zeitz's question about Being in corporations ("I mean, shouldn't we ideally be in business as well as be working on what we think is very important in our life?") an impossible ideal? Why or why not?

- What makes Being-centered leadership relevant or not relevant to your situation? Does it matter if you're religious, spiritual, atheistic, agnostic, or whatever?

PART 2

Recognition

Let the people glorify many gods,
Let them perform many rituals,
But without recognizing the truth
Of their own being,
There is no freedom,
Even in countless millennia.

ĀDI ŚAṄKARA (8TH CENTURY CE)

3

The Higher Reality of Rituals

From the false, lead me to the real,
From darkness, lead me to light,
From death, lead me to immortality.

BRIHAD-ĀRAṆYAKA UPANISHAD

The first stage in the lower bird's quest to realize the higher bird is its recognition of its current situation and the larger context of the tree that is its higher reality. In business, it is an attempt to be aware of the preoccupations of the moment and at the same time recognize the higher reality within which business is embedded. This recognition usually begins in an indistinct, tacit way that is hard to articulate initially but gradually becomes stronger and more explicit over time.

In this chapter, by looking at the role of rituals, I will identify two key aspects of this higher reality: the larger relationships of business and the shared purpose of business leaders. I will develop these concepts more fully for business in the next chapter. The importance of rituals to ancient India (and other Axial Age civilizations) roughly paralleled that of business work to modern societies. The goal of rituals was to relate the larger context of human existence to the life of an individual human being. I illustrate this goal through my own experience with the rituals of death—some of the most important of hundreds of ancient Indian rituals.

The Rituals of Death

It is strange how death and its rituals bring us closest to a sense of timeless being. It is when someone ceases to *be* that Being itself makes most sense. I vividly remember a day in early December almost five years ago. My father had just passed away in India, and I, the elder of his two sons, had arrived the previous morning from the United States to cremate him according to Indian tradition. On that day, I had just placed a pitcher of water on my shoulder and slowly poured it behind me as I walked around my father's body. As the fire burst from the logs of the pyre and consumed the body, I felt a curious sense of detachment—what I was seeing go up in flames was not my father.

Amid the heat and crackle of the logs, the sparks that rose in the late morning sun, and the hushed features of all my relatives gathered round the fire, I sensed something different. It was a faint sense of a presence that transcended what was getting destroyed in the fire. And then a thought came quietly over me as the flames consumed the body: "Here in my evanescent feeling of something else is the ancient belief in a deathless being."

The subsequent Hindu death rituals, though excruciating in their extent, were designed to reinforce this distinction between transient body and enduring being. They lasted twelve days, with a special ceremony on the last day for the spirit that had survived the fire and would by now, according to Hindu beliefs, grow back its outer physical body. The twelve days offered food and sustenance to this spirit as it grew new limbs before beginning the journey to worlds that lay beyond.

At the center of these ceremonies was a black stone representing the great god Vishnu, the leading deity to propitiate. For these rituals, Vishnu was the manifestation of Being itself. The Garuda Purāṇa, the ancient text that is the basis for the Hindu rituals, tells that it was Vishnu himself who described the ceremony and the journey in the afterworlds to Garuda, the king of eagles. As my father's elder son, I was presiding over these rituals and the offerings to the priests who were instructing me, to my ancestors, to the gods, and ultimately to Being.

As I performed the ceremony, I found myself falling into two parallel tracks. The first was of unquestioning action, obediently following what the head priest was telling me to do. In the second, I had stepped away and was trying to make sense of how these rituals shaped my relationship with my father and my ancestors. I learned another lesson during that ceremony: the rituals deepened key aspects of my individual identity profoundly by promoting a sense of belonging that transcended time and space.

Take, for example, the creation and offering of the three rice balls in front of me that were at the heart of the ceremonies. These were *pindas*, the food offered to my ancestors that would sustain them in their heavenly abodes. When the rituals first began for my father, the rice ball closest to me was an offering to my grandfather, the one in the middle to my great-grandfather, and the one farthest away to my great-great-grandfather and all who had come before him. In these rice balls that I created during my father's death rituals was my family identity.

As I placed the first ball in front of me, I said "Kishtayya *garu*" in response to the priest's request to name my grandfather. *Garu* is a term we use as a mark of respect. But Kishtayya *garu* is really my paternal grandfather's eldest cousin. Almost eighty years ago, Kishtayya *garu* and his wife, who were childless, had approached my paternal grandfather and asked to nominally adopt his younger son, my father, as his own. His wish had been granted readily.

As I heard the priest chant hymns that have remained essentially intact for almost three thousand years, I understood why Kishtayya *garu* had adopted my father. He was looking ahead to days like this when these rituals would be performed. I gazed silently at the first rice ball before me, the one that was meant for Kishtayya *garu*. Without a son to perform these rituals and a grandson to repeat them years later, there would have been no *pindas* for Kishtayya *garu* and his wife in the lands of the ancestors, when they had to be sustained by their descendants.

Later in the ceremony, as I recombined the rice balls and then separated them again, I performed another critical part of the ritual. I spoke my father's name over the first ball of rice. The line had moved. My father had taken the place of his adopted father, who then moved to the middle. Kishtayya *garu* had gotten his wish. He was preceded by a son, as he in turn took the place of his father, who was then fed, along with all his ancestors, by the last rice ball.

It was then that the thought hit me: "When my time comes, I too will join this line and become the first oblation. I too will have a place in this lineage woven by offerings that sustained the generations."

I felt something powerful stirring inside me. I thought of it as a tug of ancient memory that reached back over the three millennia since these rituals had been created. It was a deep time scale beyond the ordinary time scales that my professional work could impact, which gave me a sense of belonging more intense than anything my professional life had to offer. It was a profound sense of identity with a lineage and also a deep purpose in sustaining it. That these rituals had been observed over hundreds of years gave me a sense of something far higher than me.

After the twelfth day, I had come to the end of these ceremonies. But I had to perform one last ritual before my father could begin his new journey. It was this final trip that I undertook for him now, sitting in an air-conditioned rental car with my uncle and my cousin as we followed the river Krishna as it flowed eastward into the Bay of Bengal.

Six months ago, as he prepared for death, my father had pulled all his children aside and told us his last wishes. He wanted his ashes to be dispersed in the same spot where he had scattered the ashes of his brother and his father many decades ago. As I heard him speak of his last wish, I had thought, "Why is he so insistent that his ashes be dispersed in this place that none of his children know?"

Identity and Meaning

Now, as I made my way with my father's ashes to the river before it merged with the sea, I felt that I understood. After his life's journey from an ancestral village to a coastal town and the premier university in the city in the north, after a shining career that took him abroad to the great intellectual and cultural centers of the world, and after all the friends he had made in other lands, he had wished to return to that which had anchored his identity all along—the small, core family of long ago that pulled at his memories as he waited to die.

It was the same shining force that animated his words and gestures when he talked of his relatives. I remembered the many hours we spent tracking down old photographs and trying to identify who it was that looked so strangely back at us, dressed in old clothes and with bare feet, their faces darkened by the sun that beat down upon their villages. He would point to them in the photographs with excitement, his voice calling me into the web of family tradition, and say, "Here are Kishtayya *garu* and his wife, and here are my father and mother on the day they got married."

When I remembered his words again, as I sat with silent tears in the car that was taking me to his body's final place, I was oddly reminded of what Nancy Reagan had said about Ronald Reagan when he was dying. She had been asked what her husband talked about toward the end, and she said something like, "He doesn't talk of us at all. He can hardly recognize us. All he talks about are his brother and his parents when he was young."

"This is the final layer of identity we peel away," I told myself, "this last layer of family we grew up with"—the brothers and sisters and the parents of our childhood when we were still new to the world. Beyond this material identity lay only Being, that silent presence I had faintly and unsurely sensed as I cremated a mortal body.

Soon the river presented itself, the mighty Krishna as it made its way to the sea. The land was rich with soil that was ideal for growing rice. We saw thatched huts and bales of hay and paddy fields stretching for miles around us. Our car jostled for space on a narrow road as trucks, tractors, and an occasional bullock cart passed us by on the other side.

We drove alongside the river for a while until it twisted away slowly into the distance. We passed through villages whose names I had memorized in childhood because they were part of my family's presence here. I was returning to the countryside of my ancestors with the pot containing my father's ashes, searching for Puligada, the Tiger's Spot. I was looking for the place where the Krishna flowed under a bridge and into the sea.

We found the place eventually, a small beachhead of sand at the foot of an old path lined by stones beside a small temple. There was not much there except for some old plastic bags carelessly strewn around and some buffaloes grazing lazily by the water that had formed in pools under the bridge. I felt a twinge of disappointment as I slowly descended the thorn-strewn path to the water. I had expected to find something more elaborate and organized, perhaps a platform where the cremation rituals could be completed.

We found an open spot that was free of animal dung and thorns. My uncle and I slowly lowered ourselves into the river and watched quietly as the ashes from the immersed pot dispersed in the waters. It was time to let go, to release the last remnants of a body that had traveled sixty years ago from its ancestral land to places beyond the ocean before returning to flow down to the sea.

For ancient Indian and many other civilizations of the Axial Age, rituals represented some of the most important work that could be done in life. Because they were sacred, they required great preparation from the person performing them. Without this preparation and careful execution, the appropriate meaning of the rituals could not be obtained. If done improperly, grave consequences could ensue for the person who performed the rituals, as well as the community.

As I recall my experience around the death rituals, I am reminded of how they provided me with a firsthand glimpse—however faint and uncertain it was—of the differences between the material body and timeless being, between what rituals needed to be done precisely and at the right moment and the meaning those rituals represented beyond space and time. It was this higher meaning—of lineage and ancestors, of propitiation and nurturing, of responsibilities and effort—that gave me a sense of the larger reality within which I led my life.

I was responsible to the lineage of ancestors represented by the rice balls in the ceremony. My purpose was to preserve this lineage and to support and nurture those who came before me, even for those like me who did not believe in the afterlife, and to ensure there would be others to perform these ceremonies in the future. The purpose of the rituals was to ensure that I felt in my core this higher reality of a lineage I represented and my role in preserving and renewing it. This higher reality referred especially to the larger relationships I had with my ancestors, as well as our shared purpose over generations in nurturing everyone in the lineage.

Value to the Business Leader

Despite the considerable effort that the death rituals (and other rituals) required from the individual performing them, they provided value that far exceeded the costs. While they are far less elaborate now than they were in ancient India, they required considerable personal discipline to prepare for and conduct them, as anyone who sat cross-legged on the floor for many hours a day (and days upon end) in front of a smoke-filled fire can attest.

It was a discipline that prepared you to think of individuals before and after you, as well as levels of hierarchy within your larger context (such as family, community, society, humanity, nature, and ultimately Being). Such order and alignment was a great source of comfort in crises and disruptions, such as the death of a loved one. *Being provided the underlying explanation, source, and order behind this complexity and change.* The end result was a system that cohered across different levels and was sustained by society over millennia in India.

There are similar lessons for business work (the rituals of modern society) in an era when complexity and change have increased dramatically. Being can be an organizing principle that gives managers something to hold on to as they make difficult decisions in a challenging business environment.

Where the needs of many stakeholders must be balanced, the impacts of decisions are often unclear, and time is of the essence, Being-centered leadership could provide the broader perspective and calmness of mind to make effective decisions. Of course, the great challenge is to ensure that Being-centered norms of work do not become rigid and exclusive, which was the chief problem with rituals and the social classes of ancient Indian society.

But there is even greater value from Being than perspective and serenity. My experience with the death rituals showed me how personal value came from a sense of identity with an ancestral lineage, as well as a sense of shared purpose that gave deep satisfaction when the rituals were accomplished. This was intentional. Rituals, such as those conducted around birth, marriage, death, and a host of other events, bound human beings to one another and to Being in ancient societies. Their core purpose was to provide meaning to ordinary human life, one that was deep, consistent, and engaged with the world.

Being-centered leadership can similarly provide this identity and meaning to business work for its practitioners. This is because it can lead to a sense of vital engagement and alignment with different levels of the larger context (for example, team, company, society, humanity, nature, and ultimately Being) of a business leader.

In a fascinating discussion of the role of rituals in society, psychologist Jonathan Haidt shows how this cross-level alignment and vital engagement are key ingredients to personal happiness. As he points out, "meaning and purpose simply emerge with the [alignment], and people can get on with the business of living."[1] For Being-centered leaders, such meaning and purpose can enable happiness at work because it is naturally aligned with their identity or sense of self.

There's another way in which Being-centered leadership can be valuable. As management scholars Louis Fry and Mark Kriger point out, this journey of centering in Being becomes a source of inspiration for every other aspect of business leadership, such as spiritual perception, moral sensitivity, leadership values, and leadership skills and actions.[2] As a result, Being helps guide these aspects, even as it transcends them in ways that people who are spiritual, religious, agnostic, or even atheistic can relate to. Through Being, all levels of business leadership could improve. This is why Being-centered leadership is the highest level of business leadership.

Another important and comforting point to recognize is that you don't need to be fully centered in Being to see these benefits. The journey itself leads to profound changes, as my own experiences have shown me clearly. While many of these personal experiences are described in the next part, here I want to describe one simple but important personal benefit—*an increase in personal productivity.* It is a benefit that I first recognized when the Upanishads came into my life in the last year of my doctoral studies. They enabled me to finish my studies in the limited time that was available before I had to take up the academic job that awaited me.

Even now, I don't quite know what it was about the contemplation of Being that made me work so productively. Perhaps it was the clarity that it brought to my mind because it stilled a deep restlessness that distracted me from my work. Perhaps it allowed me to hold in perspective and even transcend the perfectionism and other barriers that got in the way of finishing my work.

In the years since, this journey has provided me with a higher sense of belonging and purpose—my own higher reality—that connected me to the higher bird of Being. It is of profound value and affects everything I do, however incomplete my journey has been.

Business work has the potential to be as helpful for us as rituals were for our ancestors. If business is to reconnect with the world, Being-centered leadership requires us to reflect on two fundamental beliefs about the larger context, or higher reality, of business: What are the larger relationships of business, and what is the shared purpose of business leadership? In the next chapter, I describe what the Upanishads have to say about this higher reality of business.

TWEETS

- Rituals convey a larger sense of relationship and shared purpose; they can relate human beings to their larger context of existence.

- Being is an organizing principle for managers to hold on to as they make difficult decisions in the midst of complex and rapid change.

- Like rituals, Being-centered leadership can provide a larger identity and meaning to business work for its practitioners.

- Larger meaning and shared purpose enable happiness for Being-centered leaders as work aligns with their identity or sense of self.

- Being inspires other aspects of leadership, such as spiritual perception, moral sensitivity, values, and leadership skills and actions.

SEEDS

- If you've experienced the death of a loved one, what rituals did you observe and how did they affect your sense of larger relationships and shared purpose with others?

- How does your work provide you with a larger meaning to life, including a sense of larger relationship or shared purpose? If it doesn't, what are some ways that it could?

- How would a sense of larger relationships or shared purpose at work make you more secure, happier, or more productive or help in other ways?

- How would a sense of larger relationships or shared purpose inspire other aspects of the leadership you could show at work?

4

The Higher Reality of Business

When the gods made a sacrifice
With the Man as their victim, . . .
From his breath the wind was born.
From his navel came the air,
From his head there came the sky,
From his feet the earth,
The four quarters from his car,
Thus they fashioned the worlds.

RIG VEDA[1]

In the quest to realize the higher bird, the lower bird first needs to lift its gaze from the preoccupations of the branch and fruit below and recognize the higher reality of the tree above. For business leaders, as I suggested in the previous chapter, this means recognizing the higher relationships of business and the shared purpose of business leadership itself. Let's consider first what the Upanishads say about these higher relationships and shared purpose for human beings, especially as they relate to nature. I'll then apply these lessons to business leadership.

Higher Relationships

The Upanishads maintain that humanity has been inextricably connected to nature from the very beginning. To emphasize this point, they retain a key image from the Vedas: the world as created from the sacrifice of the primeval being. In the Vedas, this primeval man (*purusha*) was Prajāpati, the Lord of Beings, who existed before the creation of the universe. The gods sacrificed this primeval being, and the natural elements were produced from his body, as the opening verse of this chapter describes.

This message of a person being inextricably connected to nature is also found in the Brihad-āraṇyaka Upanishad. An anecdote about the inimitable sage Yājñavalkya is particularly relevant.[2] At the time of the story, Yājñavalkya has reached the age when the joys of being a householder have paled against the urgings of a different purpose. He decides to leave his two wives, Maitreyī and Kātyāyanī.

As he is about to depart, Yājñavalkya calls Maitreyī, his favorite wife, to his side and says, "I am about to leave, my dear. I want to distribute my wealth between you and Kātyāyanī." Maitreyī asks, "If all the world's wealth were mine, would I become immortal?" The sage replies, "No, my dear. You would only have lived the life of a wealthy person. Immortality does not come through wealth." Maitreyī pointedly replies, "What is the use of having vast wealth when it does not bring me nearer to immortality? Instead, tell me what is most important to know about this world."

Much pleased, Yājñavalkya replies, "It is not for the sake of the husband that the husband is dear, but it is for the sake of one's true self in the husband that the husband is dear. It is not for the sake of the wife that the wife is dear, but it is for the sake of one's true self in the wife that the wife is dear." Yājñavalkya speaks of the love for a child, for wealth, for priestly and royal power, and even for the world, other beings, and the gods themselves in the same manner: they are all dear to us because the same universal self (Ātman) is in all of them.

Just as smoke emanates from a fire, all waters eventually reach the ocean, all sensations of touch emerge from the skin, all smells converge in the nostrils, and all tastes originate in the tongue, so too do all beings originate in the Ātman. This earth, this water, this fire, this air, this sun, these four directions, this moon, this lightning, this cloud, this space, this law, this truth, this humanity, and this individual self—all these are the honey for all beings and all beings are their honey.

The same universal self that resides in all these elements resides also in all beings and is therefore identical to the foundational reality, or Being. *When we destroy nature, we are destroying an integral part of ourselves.*

These stories from the Upanishads, composed almost three thousand years ago, describe two different aspects of the vital connection and interdependence between humanity and nature. First, humanity is organically connected to nature in the sense that our bodily parts are the parts of nature, as described in the sacrifice of the primeval man. Second, this organic connection is because of the same universal self (identical to Being) that is common to us.

Shared Purpose

Shared purpose transcends the individual purpose that is unique to a particular person; it describes the common endeavor of human beings. The core message of the Upanishads is that shared human purpose depends on a person's stage of life,[3] while the manner in which a person accomplishes this shared purpose is particular to that person's circumstances. According to the Upanishads and the older Vedic culture in which they were embedded, the ideal life of every human being had four stages (*āśramas*)[4]: student, householder, forest dweller, and world-renouncing ascetic.

Importantly, each stage had its own set of shared purposes, in addition to the individual purposes of the person at that stage. As a student, a person learned the Vedas, gained greater self-control, served the teacher, and prepared for life's responsibilities, all with the shared purpose of acquiring knowledge. As a householder, a person married, brought up a family, engaged in an occupation, and supported the community to the extent possible, all with the shared purpose of acquiring wealth and pleasure.

As a forest dweller, a person restrained material desires and attachment to family as much as possible and engaged without vested interests with everyone, all with the shared purpose of serving society. As an ascetic, all links to family, occupation, service to society, and so on, were renounced, all with the shared purpose of achieving complete freedom (*moksha*) from earthly attachments and desires.

It is important to recognize that the Upanishads did not deny the human purposes of pursuing wealth and pleasure. In fact, they explicitly encouraged them, especially at the householder stage. But such pursuits had their limits and would inevitably become less attractive. This drop in attraction picked up momentum during the forest-dweller stage, when the shared purpose shifted to serving everyone in society more fully. This was the stage when the focus on serving family and self in the householder stage was balanced by a focus on serving society.

At the last stage, that of an ascetic, every individual purpose was also renounced and the only desire that remained was for *moksha*, which was the desire to fully realize the Ātman. It was the last of the personal duties that remained, and its goal was to completely transcend the life of a human being and its limitations. It was no longer about balance between individual and shared purpose since *moksha* was the only purpose that remained. The lower bird in the tree of life had now become one with the Ātman, the bird of all-embracing compassion.

With this highest kind of freedom, a person fulfilled his final duty to himself, his family, his society, humanity, nature, and Being. However, before I relate these stages of life to business, let me hasten to say that I am *not* suggesting that business leaders become ascetics and solely pursue *moksha*! It would be the end of business. The journey of Being-centered leadership culminates with the lower bird seated *next to* the higher bird, rather than becoming one with it, in the tree of business life.

The Higher Reality of Conventional Business Leadership

Since business is an institution that is created by and composed of humans, human reality can and should inform business reality because of the Upanishadic principle of correspondence. For a Being-centered leader, it is important that the higher reality of business align with and promote a larger human reality since business is embedded within humanity. From the viewpoint of a Being-centered leader, how good is this alignment currently? The answer depends on the higher relationships and shared purpose imputed to business leadership.

If we think of nature as being fundamentally unconnected to business, then this separation enables us to think of it as little other than a resource for business. Similarly, if humanity is mainly a provider of human resources for a business, then one set of human resources is substitutable by others and almost all human resources are potentially substitutable by technology. As a result, humanity and nature become means to material ends rather than ends in themselves.

If the larger context is assumed only to be a source of resources, the shared purpose of business leadership is to maximize the efficiency of resources and substitute them when they decline in availability. The resources do not have value *in and of themselves*: their value is derived from their ability to efficiently enable the material ends of business. For business, these ends are typically to increase the throughput (or volume of flow) and profitability of material goods and services.

This view that nature is valuable only for the material ends of business is the hidden assumption behind the beliefs of conventional business and economics.[5] It is ultimately derived from the traditional Western view that humans have dominion over nature. The view that humanity is mainly a source of human resources for business is based on conventional models of economics and business that emphasize the labor productivity and efficiency of production. Together, these beliefs have created an economic model that separates business from its context while valuing material outputs such as throughput and profits as ends in themselves.

The consequence of such a view is that material ends get priority over less materialistic human needs, as well as the needs of nature. As I discussed at the beginning of this book, this separation of business from its larger context has created the global crises of nature, humanity, and institutional credibility today.

The Higher Reality of Being-Centered Leadership

The Upanishads enable a business leader to recognize a different higher reality of business by (1) organizing the higher relationships of business into a common framework and (2) identifying the shared purpose of business leadership and how it evolves over time, in terms of this framework. This recognition can occur through the Upanishadic concept of dharma, which deals with the organizing purpose of interconnected beings.

Dharma refers to balance, both moral and cosmic.[6] It is derived from an earlier Vedic concept called Ṛta, which described the natural order or the regularity of the universal process.[7] Because of Ṛta, the world was orderly, night followed day, the seasons had their interdependent purpose, and there was a cosmic balance between the worlds of humans and the gods.

Simply put, Ṛta was what was right for the world (the English word *right* has the same Indo-European root as Ṛta), and dharma was the manifestation of Ṛta in particular contexts, such as humanity, societal class, family, or an individual. All these different components had to be in harmony with the natural law for universal order to prevail.

The concept of dharma as balance has many parallels to recent findings in science, which makes it relevant today. For example, neuroscience research emphasizes the vital role of biological homeostasis in holding living beings together.[8] For a living being to survive, its body needs to maintain a large variety of conditions—such as temperature; acidity as measured by pH; levels of a variety of chemicals; amounts of fundamental nutrients such as sugars, fats, and proteins; and many others—within specific ranges. The process for achieving this balance is called *homeostasis*. Biological homeostasis is therefore a direct biological analog to dharma as the principle of dynamic balance that holds a living being together.

If balance is vital to human bodies, human life, and human societies, can it be extended to businesses too? Indeed, it can. In one of the most important research efforts on visionary companies, management consultants Jim Collins and Jerry Porras noted that highly successful companies maintain a dynamic balance between preserving their core ideology and stimulating a drive for progress.[9]

Creating the means to simultaneously preserve and renew this essence is vital to business success. Collins and Porras illustrated this business dynamic through the familiar Chinese symbol of yin and yang, which represented the balance within an individual and between humanity and nature.

Let us see how the dharma of business leadership helps leaders recognize the two aspects of their higher reality: its higher relationships and shared purpose.

Dharma of Business Leadership and Higher Relationships

Rather than treat nature and humanity as resources, the Upanishadic view is that humanity, nature, and business are inextricably connected to one another and to Being. By treating humanity and nature as mere resources, business damages them, its connections to them, and itself. Even a faint recognition of this higher reality sets leadership on its journey to the higher bird.

The Upanishads further say that the interconnections can be organized into a hierarchy. When applied to business, this means that business depends on the economy, which depends on humanity, which depends on nature, while all eventually are derived from and depend on Being for their existence. In other words, business is a subsystem of the economy, which is a subsystem of humanity, which is a subsystem of nature; all these subsystems are ultimately in Being.[10]

A subsystem cannot flourish if the containing system is unhealthy. This means that at the lower bounds of any balance the minimum requirements for keeping the higher systems healthy *must* be preserved. Otherwise, business activity will compromise the very foundations on which the economy and business are built.

These foundational systems of humanity, nature, and Being are like the commons from which the village derives fundamental services such as water, pasture for grazing animals, wood for fuel, recreational space, and others. When these commons are depleted, the economic life of the village collapses.

The imperative for business to preserve and renew its human, natural, and Being-centered foundations may seem obvious, but it is not so if you believe that the different systems are separate from one another and do not form a hierarchy, that the sole purpose of business is to maximize its self-interest, and that the commons can be substituted by other means. If this is the case, there really is no lower bound to these other systems. If the commons could be substituted, the material economy could grow without limit through technology, innovation, and other means.

An important way to understand the health of the different subsystems is by considering the extent of capital that is available for each of them. For a Being-centered leader, four kinds of capital truly matter, one for each of the subsystems:

- *Material capital,* which describes the material wealth produced by the business and includes the stock of material goods and services as well as physical capital and infrastructure used for production
- *Human and social capital,* which is the value of human resources and social interactions describing the humanistic wealth of the business
- *Natural capital,* which is the stock of available natural ecosystems and biodiversity for providing valuable natural goods and services
- *Being capital,* which describes the extent of business integrity, trust, and other foundational values within business

The economist Schumpeter was the first to show that *creative destruction* is at the center of free-enterprise capitalism. The term refers to the forces of novelty and innovation that enable new ideas, goods, and services to thrive while the old ones lose their appeal, thereby leading to the birth and death of companies and markets.

For a Being-centered leader, the dharma of business leadership is maintained if the forces of creative destruction are such that the different kinds of capital stay above their lower bounds at all times. When they fall below these bounds, they are at high risk of not being replenished. When this happens, the foundations of business and the economy are undermined.

Being capital is endangered when levels of trust and integrity in economic institutions such as corporations are dangerously low. Natural capital is endangered when the effects of climate change and ecosystem and biodiversity loss become irreversible. Human and social capital is endangered when the minimum survival conditions of health, education, and social connection are not met. Material capital is endangered when the basic material needs of many in society for food, water, clothing, shelter, and other essentials are neglected. It is also endangered when the material conditions of the workplace, such as pay, benefits, and physical work conditions are neglected.

For Being-centered leaders, the key is to preserve the survival conditions of capitalism while stimulating progress through the renewing power of creative destruction that competitive markets provide.

Without the preservation of the lower bounds, the economic, humanistic, natural, and Being-centered connections of business to the world eventually collapse. Without the upward push of creative destruction, those same connections stagnate. When they are all in balance, progress is sustained. Being-centered leaders therefore follow a *dharma principle* that maintains the foundational integrity and long-term survival of business. It's a simple principle to guide business work at all times: *don't fall below the lower bounds and undermine the foundations, the larger systems, while creating something new and destroying the old.*

The market forces of creative destruction work best from a foundation that is secure, not when the base itself is being undermined. In terms of the overarching symbol of the two birds in a tree, the goal of Being-centered leadership is to ensure that the tree is not being stripped completely of its fruit and that the roots are not being undermined in the lower bird's frenetic pursuit of its wants.

Dharma of Business Leadership and Shared Purpose

The dharma principle gives the organizing rule for maintaining balance among the different subsystems that describe business's connections. But it doesn't tell a business leader about which kinds of capital should be emphasized when. To make such decisions, Being-centered leaders consider the macrolevel stage of business leadership they are working within and whether their business work is promoting the shared purpose of this stage.

These macrolevel stages are different from the stages of the REAL road map for Being-centered leadership. The macrolevel stages refer to the historical evolution of business leadership since the Industrial Revolution, while the REAL road map refers to the inner journey of an individual business leader. From the viewpoint of Being-centered leadership and the stages of evolution (*āśramas*), the macrolevel external trajectory of business leadership since the Industrial Revolution has included preparation, growth, and restoration of balance.

Preparation The 1800s was a preparatory period as the Industrial Revolution picked up momentum from the previous century, first in England and then in the rest of Europe and America. Business leadership was in its student stage, when it was learning the lessons needed to organize production and labor and to distribute goods and services to customers. Material capital was low at this stage because of the poor pay, benefits, and physical conditions of work. Human and social capital was low because of the relatively low industrial employment and poor social conditions in Western societies. The dharma principle with regard to material, human, and social capital was close to the lower bound.

Natural capital was high because humanity and the economy had low impacts on nature because of their small scale. Being-related capital was beginning its decline as philosophy (and its offshoot, science) increasingly became an intellectual effort or a way to solve particular problems, rather than a way to live one's life, which is how it had been interpreted in ancient Western philosophy.[11] Business leadership's primary purpose in this stage was to learn the lessons for growing material, human, and social capital above the lower bounds.

Growth The 1900s was a period of tremendous growth in material capital in the West. Business leadership moved into its householder stage, where its chief purpose was to acquire material wealth and pleasure and distribute it to society's members. Techniques of mass production and distribution were perfected, and the modern business organization took shape in the early 1900s. The use of technology accelerated in the second half of the century. Information technology drove this growth even further in the last two decades, and the availability of material goods and services rose sharply, especially after 1950.

Human and social capital rose rapidly throughout much of the century, creating economic and social well-being for many. However, its growth began to slow and even flatten in the last three decades of the twentieth century as economic and social disparities in society began to increase.[12] The chief challenge of this stage was the violation of the dharma principle with regard to natural capital.

Creative destruction had resulted in huge growth in material capital, but this burst of wealth had come at the cost of natural capital. By the end of the century, the stock of natural capital was declining rapidly to levels below their lower bounds.[13] The public's trust in business and its integrity began to decline as markets got hypercompetitive, the financial sector rose to dominance, and questionable business practices had increasingly large and systemic impacts.

Restoration of Balance At the beginning of the twenty-first century, business leadership finds itself in a crisis. Increases in material capital continue to destroy natural capital, and many of the natural limits are approaching irreversibility. Of the nine kinds of planetary limits identified by the Stockholm Resilience Institute, we seem to have crossed three of them (climate change, biodiversity loss, and interference with the nitrogen cycle) already and are rapidly approaching the limits for four others (freshwater use, changes in land use, ocean acidification, and interference with the global phosphorus cycle).[14]

Human and social capital has continued to decline steeply as business and capitalism's ability to distribute wealth equitably is eroding.[15] Being capital has declined as business and capitalism's integrity is under threat. Business leadership is often seen as encouraging individual self-interest even at the cost of humanity and nature, and at the cost of integrity and trust.

For a Being-centered leader, if business leadership is to be rejuvenated, its shared purpose must no longer be to focus overwhelmingly on material capital but to restore economic balance (dharma) among business, the economy, humanity, nature, and Being. In other words, the focus on growing material capital, which could be justified when other kinds of capital were available, is not compatible with the dharma principle in this century.

To restore the dharma of business leadership, business leaders need to systemically prioritize restoring human, social, natural, and Being capital so that the foundations of business are not undermined. Business leadership needs to find its own version of the forest-dweller stage, where the focus is on restoring balance in the world. This means a determined focus on *restorative* economic growth rather than destructive growth that results from prizing material capital above all other types of capital. This focus is especially relevant to natural capital that cannot be easily restored.[16]

All other purposes are secondary to this shared purpose of restoring the larger systems (or foundations) that is the higher reality in which business is embedded. *Every purpose that damages this shared purpose is not dharma.*

TWEETS

- The larger reality of business is that it is embedded within humanity and nature.

- The hidden assumption of conventional business and economics is that nature is valuable only as a resource for the material ends of business.

- Business is a subsystem of the economy, which is a subsystem of humanity, which is a subsystem of nature, which is a subsystem of Being.

- The dharma of business leadership is to preserve the lower bounds of the larger systems that contain business while creating something new.

- All other purposes are secondary to the shared purpose of restoring the larger systems (or foundations) in which business is embedded.

SEEDS

- How does the relationship among business, the economy, humanity, and nature affect the limits to which an economy can grow?

- What qualities or metrics would you include in natural and Being capital? How would you distinguish them from human, social, and material capital?

- What would a set of systems where the dharma principle holds look like? How would the dharma principle change the priorities of the senior leaders in your organization?

- How would you implement the shared purpose of restorative growth in your own individual job or in your group? What gets in the way of doing so?

PART 3

Experience

Consciousness is this world's eye,
It is this world's foundation,
Consciousness is Being itself.

AITAREYA UPANISHAD

5

Engaging
with Experience

Take this great bow of the Upanishads,
Place in it an arrow sharp with veneration,
Draw it with mind fully engaged,
Know the target as Being, my friend.
MUNDAKA UPANISHAD

B y now, the lower bird has some recognition of the higher bird;
it has a larger sense of relationship and shared purpose for
itself. Even if it is only at a tacit level, this recognition can be
a powerful force and a source of inspiration and energy for a business
leader. The next stage in the REAL road map makes this recognition more tangible and explicit through experiences that fully engage
the heart and mind of the business leader. The need to engage is
important, as shown in a story involving the sage Yājñavalkya and a
great king in the Brihad-āranyaka Upanishad.[1] It has been called the
supreme teaching of the Upanishads and says that to make progress,
we must genuinely desire to engage fully in the quest for the higher
bird.[2]

The Supreme Wisdom

Once long ago, Yājñavalkya came on one of his periodic visits to
the court of King Janaka, the wisest and most powerful ruler of his
times. He brought with him a supreme wisdom that he intended
to keep to himself.[3] When the two were seated, King Janaka began

his questioning, intent on shaking loose this wisdom from a reluctant sage.

The king asked, "What is that light that guides a person well in this life?"

Yājñavalkya answered, "The sun is this guiding light, your majesty. One sits, moves around, ventures forth, and works under this light."

"Very true; it is as you say," said the king, "but what happens when the sun has set?"

"It is the moon, your majesty," replied Yājñavalkya.

The king persisted, "It is just as you say, Yājñavalkya. But what is that light when the moon has set?"

In this way, through a continuing battle of wits, the crafty Yājñavalkya and the persistent king went through the examples of fire, speech, the self that is present in us when we are awake, and the self that is present when we dream. At each example, the king promised great wealth to Yājñavalkya as a reward for the wisdom that liberates a person from worldly constraints.

Eventually, the king said, "I will give you a thousand cows as a gift, but you will have to tell me an even greater wisdom!" At this, Yājñavalkya knew that the king had cut him off from all his exits. So he began his final explanation of the steady light that guides a person in life.

After discussing how the universal self (Ātman) transcended the life and death of a person, he said, "As a man acts, so he becomes. As he performs good actions in this life, he becomes good. If he performs bad actions, he becomes bad. . . . From desire comes resolve, and from resolve comes action. And action becomes the man. . . . For the person who is free from desires, except the desire for the Ātman, there comes true freedom. . . . This is the ancient path, subtle and stretching far beyond our lives, which leads to the ultimate reality of Being. . . . Through this path go the knowers of Being. . . . for a person who has discovered the Ātman, what more wants could there be, what more worries lie ahead? . . . While we are still here in this world, what greater light is there to seek? Great is the destruction for the one who does not seek this light. . . . Great is the darkness for those who do not seek this reality. . . . From death to death goes the one who does not see this unity, this connectedness. . . . The one who knows the Ātman is calm, patient, untroubled, and at peace. Such a person sees all beings in this universal self, and the universal self in all these beings."

Yājñavalkya concluded, "This is the reality, O king, that I have shown to you." At this, the king offered neither great wealth as reward nor further doubt but his final and only true offering: "I give my whole kingdom and all of myself to this light."

This is the supreme wisdom of the story: the freedom from the many deaths due to the challenges of our life is worth our *full engagement* with the quest for the higher bird that is Being. Guided by this quest, there is little to fear in this world. When leaders engage fully in seeking this light, they often end up questioning long-held assumptions that shaped their previous mind-sets and behaviors.

For example, in the verses introducing chapter 2, the Isha Upanishad stresses the importance of both doing and knowing and both the tacit and the explicit. As we have seen previously, rituals were the conventional means by which humans could connect with eternal realities. This had been so for perhaps a thousand years before the Upanishads were composed and was a central feature of the Vedic age that preceded them. The immense importance of performing rituals correctly, the great personal value derived from them, and their central role in maintaining global harmony was undisputed in ancient Indian society.

For many conventional thinkers and ordinary people, it was implicitly assumed that Vedic rituals were necessary, efficacious, and crucial in ensuring individual, community, and societal success. At least for the learned classes, they were considered the most important activity that human beings could perform and therefore represented work itself. In fact, the Sanskrit word *karma* was used both for rituals and for work.[4]

A new and daring school of thought claimed that these rituals (or at least their physical performance) were completely unnecessary, that the same results could be obtained by internal reflection, such as meditation. Inner knowledge of the truth of one's own being was the means through which one could connect with cosmic realities and obtain merit.

As these ideas began to spread through the hermitage schools sprinkled throughout ancient India, this revolutionary viewpoint gradually became an implicit assumption in itself. The knowledge that came from internal reflection was obviously the one true means for knowing truth.

It is the unexamined faith in these two contrasting viewpoints, and the implicit assumptions underlying each of them, that the Isha Upanishad questions through its dramatic paradoxes—the knowing and the doing, the tacit and the explicit. In effect, through the three verses related to knowledge and rituals, the Isha Upanishad is trying to say to us "Beware of implicit assumptions that make you believe you are right! They will lead you astray if you do not recognize them."

In our contemporary context, these verses tell us that internal imagination and external work are two sources of knowledge that are *both* necessary for Being-centered leadership:

- *Introspective knowledge*, which is knowledge acquired through study, insight, reflection, meditation, intuition, or similar "imagining" means
- *Knowledge in action*, which is knowledge acquired through performing work, following procedures, undertaking service, or similar "doing" activities

The tacit assumptions that lead to an unquestioning faith in one extreme only lead to a distortion of reality.

From Tacit Assumptions to Explicit Experience

Tacit assumptions are around and in all of us, as I have learned through personal experience. In my particular case, the emphasis on scholarly learning was even more acute because I came from a tradition of teachers. My father was a professor of astronomy, and my grandfather was a high school teacher and principal.

My forefathers belonged to a community of Hindu priests, and I grew up assuming that the great goal of life was to become a scholar. In my college years, I had my own brief rebellion against this background as I ventured into an MBA, to the great trepidation of my family. Business meant uncertainty, and a business career meant a drift away from the pursuit of knowledge, especially in science.

But my rebellion was short-lived. At the back of my mind was a value system that venerated the intellect, and it reasserted itself as I applied for a doctorate in business management soon after earning my MBA. During my doctoral studies, I flirted with thoughts of leaving academia and working in industry. After all, I had been very active in my college years in extracurricular activities that required student leadership. But these experiences were not sufficient to overcome the certainty and the comfort that came from pursuing research and teaching.

Moreover, the very establishment around doctoral education was geared toward a career in academia. While the content of study was about business practices, the form and context in which the program was conducted was scholarly. The research that was considered acceptable had to meet the standards of academic rigor, while business relevance mattered much less.

All the talk of a future career was about academia. Introspective knowledge from learning and reflection about business, not the knowledge from business implementation, was what I was unconsciously venerating for all these years, despite my brief flirtation with an MBA. One simply did not go to work for a business organization after a doctoral degree. Joining academia was the right and unquestioned thing to do, since everyone else was doing so. All our professors encouraged us to become academics, and the one or two who suggested alternatives did not have much standing.

Only after I started my career as a faculty member did I begin to realize the real implications of my decision. I now spent all my time teaching about and researching business and no time at all practicing it. I had staked out one extreme of the two opposites that the Isha Upanishad was warning against. I was putting all my time into the pursuit of introspective knowledge based on reflection and reading.

For publishing in leading research journals, what mattered most was academic rigor. Methodology trumped business relevance, even if the research findings were relatively trivial. It took several years for a research paper to see daylight because it had to address all the questions about rigor that reviewers asked. When it did get published, it was hardly read by anyone in business and therefore had almost no business impact.

Throughout these years, I was haunted by the verses of the Isha Upanishad that dealt with knowledge from introspection and action. The contrast between the extreme position I found myself in and the balanced approach that the Isha Upanishad advocated was especially vivid because the content of what I was studying was business practice. This recognition ultimately drove me out of the world of academia and into one that balanced introspection and action.

Starting a company in Silicon Valley was the sustained experience by which I eventually deepened my recognition of something higher than my material self, but it was not easy. Along the way, key incidents enabled me to transition from academia to full-time entrepreneurship.

Two of these many transitional incidents were conversations that had an enormous impact on me. Like the conversation that Timberland's Jeffrey Swartz had with a troubled teen, they resulted in a human connection that accelerated my journey from recognition of a higher reality—a higher relationship and purpose—for my life's work to a deep experience of this reality through entrepreneurship.

Two Pivotal Conversations

It was mid-1997 and the dot-com boom was in progress. It was one of the most exciting years for entrepreneurs in a long while. I had just returned from a conference of entrepreneurs in Silicon Valley, and I had decided that I was not going to be left out of this excitement. But how would I make this transition? Who would fund me or even hire me for the high-tech start-up experience I wanted? After all, I was an academic who had spent the last dozen years in research and teaching. All my skills seemed useless for entrepreneurship.

There was another way to leave academia: I could apply to consulting companies that might be interested in my background, work with them for a while, and then start my own company. After all, consulting required thought leadership, and I confidently thought I had plenty to offer. Unfortunately, every consulting company I applied to felt I had spent too many years in academia and had not worked enough with large corporations. After months of trying, I began to get desperate. It seemed that there was no way out.

Eventually, one company was interested. It seemed that former academics were welcome. I interviewed with the vice president of consulting and was fortunate to get an offer. The job involved extensive traveling, but I could be based out of Silicon Valley, the very place I wanted to be.

I was confident enough to ask for a larger salary and more stock options, even though I was worried that this was going to wreck the deal. The VP hesitated at first but then promised to talk to the CEO and see if the offer could be upped. Much to my delight, a few days later he said that he was successful. I had the salary and options I wanted and I needed to confirm my acceptance over one last call.

The day before the call, my wife left for Los Angeles, and I was left alone to take care of my year-old son. He had been having problems in the past few months in doing what children his age were supposed to do: he was unable to turn over by himself, his muscle tone wasn't typical (as his pediatrician put it), and he had a slowness about his movement and expression that was deeply worrying.

With every stirring of his sleeping body and labored breathing, I realized that as I traveled in my new job, I would not be there with him most of the time in the coming years. However exciting this opportunity was, it was presenting itself at the wrong time. My infant son could be having real problems with his health, and I would largely be missing from his life.

When the call came at eight o'clock the next morning, I did not know how to tell the VP that I was turning down the very offer I had wanted. As the words rushed out of me in a jumble of awkwardness, I felt foolish and very self-conscious. I was talking to him of my son as though he were a doctor whom I was pouring out my concerns to.

After I finished haltingly, there was a long pause at the other end.

The VP finally said, "I'm very sorry your son is having these problems. I can see why you can't take the job because of the travel."

As I began to thank him for his understanding, he said something I remember to this day: "I have the same concerns you have about consulting. I have a four-year-old daughter who is still not talking. My wife and I are very worried about her. I often think I should find a job that will get me back home every night."

With this admission from him, our relationship changed completely. No longer was he the business executive with whom I had interviewed. We spoke directly to each other as two concerned fathers, worrying about the impact of their jobs on their children and their family life. He had found a way to step out of his business persona and confide his very human concerns to me.

Perhaps it was my stumbling awkwardness that had struck a chord with him, or perhaps it was the genuine concern in my voice. Whatever it was, he had reciprocated in far greater measure by confiding what he needn't have at all. After all, he hardly knew me. But he had found a way to connect to the higher bird in him.

His willingness to establish a human connection that transcended the business nature of our relationship left a deep imprint on me. After I put down the phone, I knew that I was no longer looking at full-time consulting as my way out of academia. Instead, I decided to relocate to Silicon Valley by finding a position there that would be less demanding on my family but allow me to explore my options.

Within a year of the phone call, I was in an academic job in Silicon Valley in the middle of the entrepreneurial epicenter of the world. My son turned out to be fine eventually—he had just taken his time in acquiring age-appropriate skills.

At this time, another pivotal conversation provided me with a sense of what my future would be if I continued in academia. It was early 1999. I had gone back and forth over whether to leave academia or not. In desperation, I reached out to several people for advice. The common answer was that I should take the option that was less risky: wait for tenure and then do whatever I wanted to do on the side, as many others had done. But I just couldn't come to terms with this low-risk approach because it only pushed the can down the road.

I arranged a meeting with a widely respected chaired professor in the business school, a person who had impressed me with his gentle and wise manner. I did not know him well, but I wanted to get his thoughts on what his life was like now that he was very successful and established. He was very sympathetic to the dilemma I was facing. I asked him what life after tenure meant for academics in their middle age.

"There are only about half a dozen or so faculty I know who are in their fifties who continue to focus on research. The rest either do nothing at all or consult or do service through committee work," he said.

Emboldened by his frankness, I asked, "Do you have any regrets now that you are a chaired professor?"

His answer was direct and honest: "I wish I'd had more of an impact on my field."

I inquired further, "What is your biggest challenge now that you are well-established?"

His answer astonished me. He said simply, "Boredom."

After a lot of research had been done, after all the classes that could be taught had been taught, and after all the committee work that had to be done had been done, many of the colleagues he knew were simply bored with what they did. It seemed that the great security of academic tenure had its ever-present shadow—a sense of stasis, of life dribbling away in trivia, especially in the midst of the excitement of entrepreneurial energy in Silicon Valley. It was no wonder that tenure was thought of as "golden handcuffs" by many professors I knew.

I was now convinced that I had nothing to lose, even if I were to fail as an entrepreneur. On one side lay lasting regret and ennui, on the other, the excitement of engaging fully with something I had long wanted to do. Shortly thereafter, I applied for and was granted a leave of absence by the dean of my business school, a man of great integrity and compassion. He understood what I was aspiring to do and was willing to let me try it.

And so I took the plunge and left academia to start my own high-tech company. While I knew that start-up life was going to be difficult, little did I realize that my experiences in the next decade would be the most difficult, intense, and exhilarating of my life. These years of first-time entrepreneurship became the crucible in which my earlier dim recognition of a higher reality for myself were deepened and enriched.

Through this decade-long experience of entrepreneurship, I found a way to deeply recognize the higher relationships and shared purpose of my own life's work. The lower bird in me began to focus less and less on the seemingly sweet fruit on the surrounding branches and more so on the climb to higher branches. The tacit recognition of a higher reality I was dimly aware of in my years in academia became explicitly embedded in a deep experience I will always own, as I describe next.

The Dim Recognition Made Explicit

There is a moving episode in the first chapter of the Bhagavad Gītā, an ancient Indian philosophical text that is often considered an Upanishad. In it, the warrior-hero Arjuna tells his divine charioteer Krishna that he does not want to fight in the great battle that is about to begin. Arrayed against him are his relatives, teachers, and friends on the battlefield of Kurukshetra, near the modern Indian capital of New Delhi.

Like many people of Indian origin, I have been fascinated by the symbolism of this setting: a great warrior, unconquerable in battle and equipped with the accouterments of war but on his knees in despondence at the carnage to come. "My bow Gandiva falls from my hands," Arjuna says, "my skin burns everywhere; my mind is confused and I cannot stand, as I see bad signs of what is to come, O Krishna."

Krishna is the full human incarnation of the Ātman. The scene (as well as the rest of the text) is an allegory for the internal conversation within us between the two birds in the tree of life—Arjuna's reluctance to fight undoubtedly reflects the worldly anxieties of the lower bird. At the end of the text, Arjuna decides to pick up his great bow, Gandiva, and commence the battle he had spent years thinking about and preparing for. In this spirit, I named my start-up Gandiva.

I was fascinated by Arjuna's hesitation to fight because it mirrored my own long hesitation and doubt in becoming an entrepreneur. I had long aspired to start a company because of the knowledge running a business provided and the financial independence it could provide if successful. But I had developed an even more important reason that had to do with my own sense of my higher reality—of the being I wanted to become—in the previous decade as an academic, when I was immersing myself in the Upanishads.

Every time I stumbled with the start-up and imagined the great bow slipping from my hands, my aspiration to become this kind of person—*one who combined introspection and action while standing and fighting alongside others in the face of great adversity*—gave me silent consolation. I was seeking a freer, calmer, happier, more secure sense of myself, beyond the obvious material wealth that a successful entrepreneur would have. Ironically, material wealth seemed the means through which this higher sense of self could be obtained!

TWEETS

- When leaders engage fully in seeking Being, they end up questioning long-held assumptions behind previous mind-sets and behaviors.

- Introspective knowledge from reflection and knowledge in action through doing are *both* needed for Being-centered leadership in business.

- Unexpected human connection at work can accelerate one's journey from recognition of a higher reality to a deep experience of this reality.

- Intense settings have the potential to be the crucibles in which our sense of a higher reality of our work can be deepened and enriched.

SEEDS

- What are some hidden assumptions underlying your mind-sets and behaviors that affected the kind of work you chose in your life?

- Describe an example at your work where an unexpected human connection revealed a higher reality to you (that is, something you really care about).

- In your work, is there a balance between introspection and action? Does it matter to you? Why or why not?

- Do you see your current work as a means to a calling, a way to build a career, or a job that allows you to pursue deeper interests outside work?

6

Deepening the Experience

Death and rebirth take place in our consciousness
Therefore keep the mind pure
For one becomes one's consciousness:
This is the eternal mystery.
MAITRĪ UPANISHAD

The journey of the lower bird to the higher bird accelerates when the lower bird has deep experiences that enrich its vision of the latter. Such experiences can be further enabled if we view business leadership as a field of consciousness that mediates the interactions between the corporation and the business leader. Everyone in the corporation has a special role in business leadership, just as every subsystem in our brain has a special role in our human consciousness.

If business has to transform itself, this field of consciousness needs to change first. Moreover, because leaders contribute to this field in ways unique to them, the experiences that change them are also special to them. In my case, the experience of Gandiva as an early-stage start-up had a deep and special impact on my own journey.

Considering the vantage point of the early-stage entrepreneur has several advantages. During the initial stages when the company is being formed, the founder (or founding team) has an overwhelming impact on the nature and performance of the start-up. In turn, the founder's sense of self is heavily affected by the start-up, as any founder will attest. Early-stage start-ups are also one of the riskiest, most uncertain, and most stressful of corporations. As a result, business leadership in a start-up becomes a vivid and dynamic field in which the beliefs, values, vision, and actions of the founder shift considerably under intense pressure.

In navigating this maelstrom of a field in my own particular way, I nonetheless learned three generalizable lessons of Being-centered leadership.

Lesson 1: We Aspire to a Higher Sense of Self through Business

Business is a key means through which individuals *imagine* opportunities to develop a higher sense of self that is special to them. For example, they may think of corporate work as a way to be productive and competent in their domain of expertise, as well as serve as mentors to others in their profession. They may also aspire to deeply engage with and serve their local communities through their work. This higher sense of self is not the same as the universal self (Ātman) but one that is closer to it than the material self. Forging these connections to others and to nature moves us forward on the journey to Being.

Especially in start-ups (and increasingly in many larger corporations), individuals pour more of their time and aspirations into business work than any other activity, including sleep. Their financial security and self-esteem are crucially dependent on what happens to them in the workplace. Business leadership that fails to grasp this connection between corporations and the higher aspirations of individuals loses a special opportunity for motivating loyalty and engagement from employees. By recognizing this potential, leadership has access to a powerful source of inspiration for organizational and personal success.

But you don't have to form a start-up to acquire this deeper experience. There are simpler and less anxiety-laden ways to do so. One of the most common in business is through *evaluation*. When used for nature, evaluation gives you the economic costs of the dependencies and impacts of business on nature. The same logic can be extended to the dependencies and impacts of business on humanity, which is a really hard task because we are dealing with people. I think one of the biggest changes in business as usual will come when valuing the services provided to business by nature and humanity becomes an integral part of financial reports. This area, called *integrated reporting*, tries to value human, social, and natural capital in addition to material capital.[1]

When integrated reporting becomes standard practice (which I think is at least a decade away), a centuries-old accounting system that does not measure the full dependencies and impacts of business on humanity and nature will get transformed profoundly. When these connections get valued explicitly, they become valuable to business and therefore worth preserving.

Lesson 2: Leadership Is the Field on Which Our Material Self Casts Shadows

If business provides great opportunities for individuals to aspire to a higher sense of self, then there are also vast shadows cast by our *current* material self on the field of business leadership. I learned painfully through Gandiva that these shadows originated in my own insecurities and those of others on the leadership team, especially during start-up initiation. To understand these shadows, you should understand the business context of Gandiva.

The turn of the millennium was the time when the dot-com bubble was nearly at its peak. Start-ups that pursued exciting new technologies were receiving extraordinary valuations, even when they had no real customer base and showed no discernible path to profitability. It was in this context that I had just left academia and was exploring the kind of company I wanted to start. I was naturally drawn to Internet technologies, given the excitement around them among investors and the general public.

But there was an even deeper reason behind it. The capabilities the early investors and I visualized were advanced Internet-based services for technology professionals in their work. These services would be provided through some exciting new web-based platforms that comprised data repositories, analytical applications, and software features that were ahead of their time. It was indeed exciting stuff! We felt very confident that we could pull this off.

But now as I consider these early years, I realize that we had propped our ladder against the wrong wall. It was not just because the whole dot-com market collapsed within a year of Gandiva's founding. Nor was it because the particular services we initially proposed were not very valuable to technology professionals. Rather, it was mainly because the market niche in which we chose to operate did not suit our capabilities. It reflected our *insecurities* rather than playing to our strengths.

My team and I were trying to create sophisticated new technology-based solutions, even though our real strengths were in *business* solutions. While management was my real interest and strength, I had nurtured a subconscious feeling that technology was much more exciting and *real* and therefore had to be cultivated, even if I did not find it very appealing.

Naturally, this allure of technology runs deep and wide in Silicon Valley. As a result, many start-ups and leadership teams gravitate immediately to creating exciting new technologies. Many do so because technology is their real strength. But many others venture into this area because it represents an unstated weakness that they wish to overcome. These insecurities often sweep them up in the glamour of technology, while they would have been better off creating business offerings that matched their core strengths.

Start-up experience confirms the truth in positive psychology's core finding that success comes from being grounded in your strengths rather than in trying to overcome your weaknesses.[2] Business leadership develops its strengths through sustained exposure to the customer's world that it comes to understand well.

The absence of such expertise in customer domains leaves business leadership with a lack of understanding of customer problems and solutions. It then does not have a deep and clear awareness of the value that it brings to customers in their domain. Without this clear sense of customer value and knowledge, business leadership has a hard time staying still and developing a persistent vision.

The consequences of this lack of expertise were profound for Gandiva during its formation and persisted in its growth subsequently. I was drawn, like many others during the dot-com boom, to exciting new areas of online, Internet-based opportunities that were opening up every week. But in retrospect, I realize that I did not have the deep expertise that was needed in the customer and technology domains that underlay these opportunities.

This expertise was also lacking in the management team that comprised the business leadership in the early stages of Gandiva. We were proposing Internet-based technology solutions to business problems that we did not have much firsthand expertise with, a problem common to many entrepreneurs during the dot-com years.

This lack of grounding in the customer's world and in the necessary technologies resulted in a constant churn in what we were as a company and our reason *to be* as a business. The most important way that this churn affected us was in the sheer rapidity with which we took up one business vision after another and abandoned it. This abandonment often happened when potential investors or prospective customers raised objections or when new competition entered the picture.

In this sense, we were no different from the many start-ups that were going through a similar churn in their business vision, usually drawn up in PowerPoint presentations. Since presentations are easy to change, business visions similarly proved very malleable. In the case of Gandiva, we went through seven different business visions in eighteen months before we could secure venture capital investment. In terms of Being-centered leadership, the absence of a clear sense of self for the business leadership led to a business vision that was neither persistent nor grounded.

Especially in the early stages of a start-up, the business vision is mainly implemented through its business model, which includes the value provided to customers, ways to make money and generate profits, business processes and partnerships used to deliver value, technology platforms, and other foundational elements of the business. Implementing this business model is the key action that business leadership can take in validating the business vision. In the absence of deep customer and technology expertise, investors can get mistaken for customers.

At Gandiva, this mistake translated into sustained pressure on the business's leadership, especially in the early stages, to pursue those business models that would meet the requirements of investors. If prospective investors sought markets that would grow rapidly (the famous "hockey stick" curve of growth), then we too sought markets that seemed to have this rapid escalation in growth. If they valued companies with "sexy" online technologies that were difficult to imitate by competition, then we would seek to develop these technologies, even if they were complex and challenging.

If investors valued certain kinds of initial customers (which were called *flagships*), then we would spend our efforts in acquiring them, even if it meant that we had to offer our services at a discount and be even more dependent on investments to see us through. As a result, we built our initial company around our expectations of what prospective investors thought was the right thing to do.

It was not that we were doing things that we felt were incorrect—far from it. In the absence of our own grounding, we had tacitly absorbed the values, beliefs, and expectations of the investors. We were treating them as customers who knew what needed to be done, while we should have been staking out our own truths with regard to customers and technology. We were not alone since many start-ups fall into this trap of mistaking investors for customers.

In effect, the actions that we undertook to secure our vision were really doing the opposite. They were creating a self-perpetuating cycle that merely confirmed the paper visions we had created instead of the deep learning that comes from being focused on real customers and staying within the limits of our technological competence. As business leaders, we were anchored in a false sense of self, a self that catered to our insecurities and expectations of what others wanted of us, rather than the self that was anchored in our own strengths and expertise.

It was at this direct and personal level that I learned one of my biggest lessons about business leadership: the corporation was not just the source of my aspirations for a higher sense of individual self but also the field on which my current self cast deep shadows.

Lesson 3: The Experience of Business Leadership Can Help Us Recognize Being

I have written until now of how my material self influenced Gandiva's business leadership and the kind of organization we were aspiring to be in the early stages of our funding. But the reverse is also simultaneously true—the kind of organization we were gradually becoming and our experiences in leading the start-up had a profound influence on my ability to recognize the higher bird (Ātman) in us.

Through these experiences, start-ups enable great personal transformation for individuals who comprise the leadership. The more intense and challenging the crucible of business leadership, the greater the opportunities for deepening our recognition of Being. But this influence is difficult to disentangle from the everyday anxieties of the material self.

As I go over the detailed notes that I made during this period, I am struck by the extent to which Gandiva and its business leadership became personalized for me. The company's difficulty in understanding the needs of the customers in its domain became amplified as *my* lack of domain expertise in everything I did and in everything I had ever done in my life.

The company's difficulty in generating investment or customer leads became magnified as *my* difficulty in relating to others.

The difficulties we had in recruiting and retaining new employees became *my* difficulty in working with teams and in delegating work to others. Business life had become personal, and business leadership shadowed my own sense of personal self.

I responded to these unremitting, overwhelming concerns in at least two ways. First, I planned incessantly. I constantly created different scenarios of the future, always making sure to have a worst-case scenario. The planning that I did above all was of ways to extend our *runway*, the most important term I obsessed over throughout my start-up life. It refers to the number of months that the start-up can survive without any additional funding or uncommitted revenue at current rates of spending (called *burn rate*) and with existing funds in hand.

The act of planning the future through numbers, events, imagined conversations, and anything else that I could get my mind around became both a source of temporary comfort and an obsession that created more discomfort eventually. It helped because it gave an outlet for the pressure building up in my mind. But it was only a paper model—like the business models we had churned through—and did not address the self's requirement for real and lasting comfort.

The repeated challenges of runway at Gandiva brought into sharp relief what the self's real need is. It reflects the kind of person we aspire to become: to be able to let go of the future, the regrets of the past, and the mistakes in the present and to allow the world to bring whatever it may to us. This surrender to the past, present, and future was my most difficult challenge at Gandiva.

I recognized well at a cognitive level that we were designed by evolution to respond to the future's uncertainty by imagining it in our minds and also that it is this very planning that makes us stumble in our search for happiness.[3] At every crisis related to the start-up's runway, I read and reread the many passages in the Upanishads and the Bhagavad Gītā that emphasized the sacrifice of the imaginative faculty in attaining happiness.

Nevertheless, I simply could not stop this incessant planning of the future, especially of the runway that we had. My notes are filled with the detailed plans of how the future could unfold for any particular problem. They testify to the obsessive fear that drove these plans in endless loops, an internal addiction to certainty that proved impossible to break.

But a second way in which I responded proved much more useful in the long run, even as it provided temporary relief in the present moment. Every anxiety or dissatisfaction that I had about how others and I were leading Gandiva became an opportunity for motivating myself. I would repeatedly go back to the reasons why I had started Gandiva and remind myself that these challenges (and even Gandiva itself) were not ends in themselves.

I would tell myself that these challenges were means toward self-improvement and for being prepared for a larger battle to come. These reminders and exhortations produced a heightened state of consciousness in me that I can only call *moving* in the real sense. Especially when the pressure was intense, I found myself moved from my current sense of self, which cared only about being effective in business, to one that cared about the larger context in which I had founded Gandiva.

While many of my writings and reflections from this period were naïve and sentimental, and almost all of them were certainly bad poetry, they served a crucial purpose in their ingenuousness. In the context of Being-centered leadership, this heightened state of consciousness served the role of expressing my own indistinct recognition of the golden-hued bird. Gandiva's travails now had a broader perspective from which these specific difficulties seemed less important. These reflections helped me tremendously in coping with the enormous levels of stress, uncertainty, and self-chastisement of entrepreneurial life.

This second way of coping with past regrets, current mistakes, and future uncertainties also served another longer-term purpose.

It created *Being memory*, specific ways in which I could access this heightened consciousness, especially when I was under great pressure. The repeated self-exhortations, the internal conversations with a higher self, the recall of dreams, the reminders of the motivation for starting Gandiva, the mythological stories of Gandiva and the heroes of the Upanishads and the Bhagavad Gītā, the desire for detaching from the outcomes of actions—all these became pathways of memory for expressing recognition of Being (however faint it often was) in my own unique ways.

In these ways, my general aspirations for a higher sense of myself that I had before starting Gandiva became a source for slowly assembling a better way to *experience* my recognition of Being. It became Gandiva's greatest gift to me.

Despite these experiences, I continue to struggle with the next set of practices related to Being-centered leadership: being steadily and consistently *anchored* in this recognition of the higher bird. In the next part, we turn to the different ways in which business leaders can choose to anchor themselves.

TWEETS

- If business has to transform itself, the field of consciousness created by business leadership needs to change first.

- Our business work could be a key means through which we imagine opportunities to develop a higher sense of self.

- The insecurities of our material self often cast vast shadows on the leadership we demonstrate at work.

- Our obsession over planning at work is a way to get comfortable with uncertainty as well as a stumbling block to our happiness.

- The experience of business leadership, especially in an intense setting, can help us recognize Being, however evanescent it may be.

SEEDS

- What kind of higher sense of self do you have for yourself in terms of your work? How does this higher sense of self bring you closer to a sense of Being?

- How does your current work enable you to access a higher sense of self? If it doesn't, how could it?

- What kinds of shadows do the insecurities of your own material self cast on your work and your relationships with others at work?

- Describe an experience at work where you felt a sense of deep connection to the world around you—a brief recognition of Being.

PART 4

Anchoring

In truth, all beings shine with Being's life-breath
The wise know this above all else
Anchoring in the Self, delighting in activity,
They're the best of the knowers of Being.

MUṆḌAKA UPANISHAD

7

Anchoring
in Suffering

Demon-haunted are the worlds
Filled with great darkness
To these dark worlds
Go the slayers of the Self.
ISHA UPANISHAD

The third stage in the quest to connect to the higher bird is to find a perch on the branches of the tree where a *steady* line of sight with the higher bird can be maintained. The lower bird needs to steadily and consistently *anchor* itself in a vision of the higher bird that can withstand the storms that rage around it. According to the principle of correspondence, the lower bird acquires the whole-tree perspective of the higher bird by connecting steadily to it. In the case of business, Being-centered leaders can then understand the real state of the business. This is the vision of the whole that they lack on their own.

If we are to understand why business is not whole today, we need to trace our journey back to the business schools that produce the business leaders of our world. The kind of education given in these schools has been an important factor in the global recession because it emphasized competition and techniques much more than cooperation and ethical values.[1]

Take my own experience as an MBA student thirty years ago in India. I think especially of our dormitory and of one particular evening in spring.

A Knock on the Door

I was getting ready for bed that night when I heard a frantic knocking on the door. It was a couple of my dorm mates who lived across the building in the wing above mine.

"Come quickly. There seems to be something wrong in Gopal's room."

"Is this urgent? I was about to go to sleep," I said.

"There is a horrible smell from his room, and his door is locked from the inside."

At this, my mind froze. Something seemed terribly wrong. I immediately thought of a conversation I'd had with Gopal a few days before. I had been sitting in the common room watching some of my friends play Ping-Pong. They were not particularly good at it. In fact, they were downright incompetent. I was having a great time pulling their legs over their inept play.

Out of the corner of my eye, I noticed Gopal walk in and sit silently next to me. As I continued to joke with my friends, I slowly realized something unusual. Gopal was much too quiet. He would normally offer some stinging criticism or biting put-down in a situation like this. Even after nearly two years together, he was still a rather aloof person who did not interact much with the rest of the class. When he did engage, he came across as arrogant and inconsiderate. He was remarkably intelligent but was rather impatient with others, particularly those he considered not as bright. As a result, he often found himself alone.

"Are you okay?" I asked.

"Nothing," he said.

"Is there something going on?" I persisted.

And then he made a remark that now seemed very significant as my mind froze at the thought of a locked and smelly room.

"You know all these people. I wish I did too," he said quietly—no irony, no trace of an underlying meaning, no cynicism, none of the put-downs we normally experienced from him.

There was another burst of noise from the people at the Ping-Pong table and I quickly switched my attention back to the game, with only a slight feeling within me that something was wrong.

Even now, after these thirty years, I can see him, his eyes bulging, his body bloated with decay, his hands tied with a strip of cloth and jammed into his *kurta pajamas* (an Indian style of clothing) in front, and the rope from which he dangled; even now I can smell the fear and horror that filled the room and leaked into the hallways and see and hear the hushed conversations and glances among the groups of students that had gathered as word of what happened rustled through the dorms swiftly.

I remember vividly the search for a suicide note. There was none on the desk nor on the bed, which would have been the obvious place to put it if he had intended that we hear his story. The police searched his room thoroughly the next day, after the stench of rotting flesh had cleared considerably. We hung over their shoulders and gave them suggestions for places to look.

We found it tucked away in the middle of a notebook, on one of the shelves of a large bookcase, amid other books. Perhaps he had thought, as he climbed up that terrible chair, that we would keep looking. Or perhaps he did not intend for this note to be discovered at all, for it carried an emotional expression that we had never associated with him: "I am committing suicide because I cannot bear having to go back to my previous job while others around me are getting good offers from all these companies. I also have no one to talk to about this, since I don't have any friends. Besides, I would have to pay back all the money to my company."

He was under a contract with his employer, a paper mill company—it would pay for his MBA education with the understanding that he would return to the company after graduation. We recognized the note's handwriting as definitely his, but the words were in a simple and direct style that was unusual for him. We puzzled over this, but all we could think of was that the magnitude of what he was going to do had resolved everything into a frightful clarity.

The week after his suicide was a blur. A friend and I had to deal with the autopsy that immediately followed because the circumstances of Gopal's death were considered suspicious. We had to walk through hundreds of cut-up bodies in the morgue to the one that was supposed to be his. We tipped the police attendant first to retrieve the body. The attendant was very matter-of-fact as he took the money, asking only how we were going to transport the body to the cremation center.

We used one of the school's trucks, got in front with the driver, and made our way through the crowded streets of the city. Thousands of lives bustled around us as we drove through the streets in the afternoon sun, the flies swirling in a thickening buzz around the body. At the cremation center, we placed Gopal on a bier that we then moved into the chamber where he would be burned.

We had also made arrangements to pick up his parents from the airport and take care of them while they were here. They came to the cremation center, where they huddled silently as he was consigned to the flames. I didn't know what to say to them. I suppose I was trying to find an answer to the unspoken question that haunted me throughout the ceremony: Why did I not show more sympathy for him when he was alive? There was a memorial service in the dorms the next morning where we spoke of how brilliant and confident he was and how his death was such a shock to us.

I think now that his family may have been yearning to hear something else. Perhaps they wanted to hear of the friends he had made and the kindnesses he had shown to others. Even if I had wanted to talk of kindness, I would not have known what to say. We were not kind to him nor had he been kind to us. He had an intense, competitive, and dominating style that drove many of his classmates away, although others among us were not very different. We didn't realize that this was his way of coping with his insecurities.

All we knew of him was that he found it very hard when others did better than him, whether it was in grades or in getting a job. It was the lower bird of ego in him, but many of us were in the same cage. Only his cage appeared to close more tightly and intensely around him.

Business education only intensified this sense of competitiveness and the pursuit of the high-paying or prestigious job and career, especially every spring when employers would come to our campus. This was true even in our institution, which was relatively relaxed about competitiveness when compared to other business schools that I have seen. Whatever the explanation, we didn't think we had anything to do with it.

The Lower Bird and Self-Worth

My mind goes back now to how his parents had silently collected his belongings after the cremation ceremony and gone their way far south to the town where they lived. Now that I'm a parent, I think of how hard it must have been for them to pick up the pieces of whatever remained of their lives, especially because Gopal was their only child. They must have agonized about which of his belongings to take back with them and which to keep subsequently.

I wonder how they must have felt as they carried his ashes home on the train making its slow way down the southern Indian coast and as they got off at their station. It would have been the same stop where they must have waited eagerly in earlier days to receive him (as my own parents did every time), their bright child returning for his holidays from the great city of hope in the northeast.

How did they speak of him afterward to friends and relatives; most of all, how did they explain the manner of his death? We received several letters from them in the few months we were in contact afterward, asking for a copy of his yearbook, for details of several awards that we instituted in his memory, and for memories of him that we could send them in writing.

I don't think we responded well to these requests. The lower bird in us had already moved eagerly forward to the shining corporate jobs that awaited us at the end of the semester. We were busy opening the doors to our own opportunities, doors that Gopal had sought so desperately to open before turning finally to the one that closed the world to him.

For Gopal and for many of us, our self-worth depended on the prestige of the companies we were going to join and the careers we were beginning to launch. I did not know it then, but I had just embarked on a long and unintended journey. On this journey, I would measure my self-worth by what I had accomplished compared to what my cohort members had accomplished. Like the lower bird who hops from branch to branch, finding that each sweet fruit eventually sours, anchoring in this spirit of competition—ultimately in suffering and sorrow—is not really anchoring at all.

Only now through the lens of the Upanishads do I see that I was caught in the lower branches of a great and grasping tree that stretched for many decades after I graduated. I would be spurred on by the fruit that others were discovering, even as I sorrowed over the fruit that was denied me, or I was filled with regret at branches I had not explored or those I stayed with for too long. But all this was in my future, while the world I was crossing into seemed powerful and exciting as I graduated from business school.

As for Gopal, he must have seemed on the outside looking in to this magical world, while the world he was returning to filled him with despair. His demons could only find release for him from the blinding darkness that seemed to lie ahead by slaying the grieving, lower bird. It was a final, terrible act of denying his self-worth. In my case, it took another two decades before I realized that there was a different self-worth to be sought, one that was rooted not in what I did or what I had that was better than my cohort's but who I was at my core.

Business education doesn't put this need for comparison into us. It only sharpens and elongates what is already there through its theories and techniques of management, of competitive strategy and differentiation, of the centrality of self-interest in making markets efficient, of being first with innovations, and of the importance of dominating markets and the thousand other ways in which competitiveness is enshrined. It was only to be expected that this instruction would feed our zeal for using comparison to anchor our own sense of self-worth and success.

At its core, business and personal success is defined in our education as *having more than what others have now*, which is different from having what is authentic to who you are. The great challenge of defining success through comparison is that there is never enough of it. Since someone you know (or have just gotten to know) is always likely to have more than you have now, success becomes a series of short-term quests for that which others have attained but is just outside your reach.

Even if business leaders define success through a longer-term lens, key stakeholders such as investors may see it very differently, as the experience of Indra Nooyi, the India-born CEO of PepsiCo, the global beverage, snack, and food company, vividly illustrates.

PepsiCo: Getting Too Far Ahead of Investors

Indra Nooyi became CEO of US-based PepsiCo in October 2006 and almost immediately began to emphasize both profits and purpose for the company. The shared purpose that she articulated for PepsiCo was to promote the health and well-being of its customers. Nooyi pushed PepsiCo to try to double its revenues from "good for you" products to $30 billion by 2020. These nutritious products included yogurts, dairy and fruit juices, hummus-based offerings, and other low-calorie snacks and beverages to complement the traditional calorie-heavy offerings. PepsiCo's drive during 2006–11 for a shared purpose became a symbol for how large corporations could do well for themselves as well as do good for the world.

By the end of 2011, however, investors had become increasingly restive. Many complained that PepsiCo was neglecting the beverage business and had ceded even more ground to beverage-focused Coca-Cola, especially in North American markets. Wall Street became concerned about Nooyi's strategy, as actual profits missed targets and the stock was down 1 percent during her leadership in 2006–11. PepsiCo's market capitalization had remained stuck around $100 billion in these five years.

By contrast, Coca-Cola's market capitalization had grown 51 percent to $153 billion in the same period. Investors were complaining that Nooyi had paid insufficient attention to beverages, and there were calls to split up the snack and beverage businesses into two separate companies. As far as investors were concerned, purpose was pilfering from profits rather than promoting them.

PepsiCo's board extended a strategic review in November 2011 of the company's business strategy, including its goal of growing nutritional offerings that were good for its customers. The results of the review were announced in March 2012. A management restructuring of the company was decided. A new role of president was created and filled by John Compton, previously the head of PepsiCo's Americas food division. The division included the highly successful Frito-Lay and Quaker food and snack businesses. Compton was also going to work with PepsiCo's regional groups in Asia, Europe, Africa, and the Middle East to reduce operating costs, create new products, and develop PepsiCo's brands globally. International brand leadership was going to become a major focus for the company.

Compton's previous role was filled by Brian Cornell, the president and CEO of Wal-Mart's highly successful Sam's Club division. Cornell was expected to bring the required leadership to compete with Coca-Cola in the slowing North American market. PepsiCo was going to try to regain market share by boosting its spending on advertisements by $500 million and by developing new products.

To help finance this spending, the company reduced its workforce by 3 percent and let 8,700 employees go. Investors seemed to like all these changes since shares immediately gained 1.3 percent, more than they had over the previous five years of PepsiCo's existence. It seems that business leadership had fought against investors and lost.

Is there an approach to corporate success in which business leadership can anchor itself, one that is more permanent than ephemeral, produces deep and steady satisfaction rather than the anxiety of comparison during its pursuit, and addresses the needs of a variety of corporate stakeholders rather than only investors?

It turns out that there is such an approach to business success that is consistent with Being-centered leadership. It has long been central to Upanishadic thinking and is now getting more attention in society.

TWEETS

- To understand why business is not whole today, we need to go back to the business schools that produce our business leaders.

- Business education doesn't put the need for comparison into us, but it sharpens what is already in us through its emphasis on competition.

- There is a different self-worth to be sought; it is based not on what we do or have but on who we are at our core.

- The challenge of defining success through comparison is that there's never enough. Success is a series of quests just out of reach.

- Even if business leaders define success through a longer-term lens, key stakeholders such as investors may see it very differently.

SEEDS

- How did your own education shape how you evaluate your success at work, especially in terms of competitive success?

- How important is your cohort at college to how you evaluate your own success? What other cohorts affect how you evaluate your success?

- Has your basis for evaluating your own work success changed over the years? If so, how has it changed and what has caused this change?

- How do the key stakeholders in your organization (for example, senior management, employees, and investors) define business success? How do these definitions differ?

8

Anchoring in Well-Being

Reality is Joy.
From Joy, all beings are born,
Through Joy they are sustained,
And into Joy they all return.

TAITTIRĪYA UPANISHAD

For the lower bird, anchoring in the branches of competitive comparison leads to a fragmented and distorted sense of success that is not sustainable. The end result is a constant dissatisfaction and a feeling of inadequacy that can lead to great fear and suffering. For business leaders, what is needed instead is to anchor in a kind of success that gives a far broader, more satisfying and consistent view of the higher reality of business. The Taittirīya Upanishad suggests one such anchor for Being-centered leaders.[1]

The Joy of Reality

A young boy, Bhrigu, was the son of the great teacher Varuṇa. When the time was ripe, the son approached his father and asked, "Radiant one, teach me about the mystery of reality."

The father answered briefly, "It is food, the breath of life, the eye, the ear, mind, and speech." But then he also told Bhrigu, "Reality is that from which beings come, in which they live and are nurtured, and into which they return when they die." Varuṇa then asked his son to meditate further on the subject, since instruction alone was insufficient to understand reality.

Bhrigu spent a great deal of time meditating on reality and then thought, "Reality is food since beings are born from food, are nurtured by it, and become food for others when they die." But he also knew that his knowledge was incomplete. So he approached his father and said, "Sir, teach me further about reality."

His father answered cryptically, "Seek to know reality by further contemplating it."

Bhrigu then spent more time in meditation and realized, "Reality is life's breath. Beings are born from life's breath, are sustained by it, and release themselves into it when they die." But being curious, he knew that his knowledge wasn't enough. He approached Varuṇa again and said, "Sir, teach me more about reality." His father again asked him to practice further since only through experience could reality be grasped.

Bhrigu then meditated further and practiced even greater austerities in his search for reality's meaning. He then realized successively that reality was the mind, and it was perception too, because it is through the mind and its perception that beings are born, are nurtured by them, and are thought and perceived to die. Now he felt that his learning was becoming more complete. He approached his father once more and asked, "Father, teach me about reality." Varuṇa again enjoined him to seek this knowledge by himself, through his own practice and austerities.

Bhrigu began his final meditations on the nature of reality. He then saw what reality ultimately meant: "Reality is Joy. From Joy, all beings are born, through Joy they are sustained, and into Joy they all return." Now there was no need to return to his father for further instruction, for Bhrigu had realized the highest vision of Being, which is that Joy (rather than fear) should be our anchor. As for Bhrigu, he became a great sage of the Upanishads and was enshrined in Indian mythology as a star that guided many seekers in their quest for reality.

Joy (*ānanda*) completes the Upanishadic trinity that comprises Being. First comes recognition of the existence of this higher reality (*sat*) of Being, then comes the experience that is the higher consciousness (*chit*) of this reality, and then comes the joy (*ānanda*) that sustains this awareness. The trinity of reality, consciousness, and joy as a way to describe Being is a simple yet profound relationship that can be applied to human beings as well as corporations. The great difference between pleasure and joy is central to how business success should be defined. Pleasure is more immediate and short-term, while joy is a *sustained delight* that includes both the present and the future.

Sustained Delight

In terms of the REAL road map, the Upanishadic notion that Being comprises reality (*sat*), consciousness (*chit*), and joy (*ānanda*) can be reinterpreted as follows. When business leaders recognize a higher reality for their business, everyone experiences their leadership as the higher consciousness of the business. Business leaders can then anchor in the vision of creating sustained delight for all the stakeholders of the business.

The concept of sustained delight lets Being-centered leaders ask important questions with regard to key stakeholders such as customers, employees, investors, and society. These questions include, What are the offerings to customers that can delight them on a sustained basis? What are the workplace conditions and interactions that can delight employees on a sustained basis? What are the returns to investors that can delight them on a sustained basis? What are the kinds of interactions with society that can delight the public on a sustained basis? While there are trade-offs in answering these questions, broadening the context beyond the immediate demands of customers or investors is a courageous but necessary act.

For a Being-centered leader, these questions can also be applied to the connection between the lower and higher birds of each kind of stakeholder. For example, they can ask, To what extent does the business enable *customers* to nurture their material self and connect to their universal self, as well as connect to humanity and nature? To what extent does the business enable *employees* to nurture their material self and connect to their universal self, as well as connect to humanity and nature? Similar questions can be asked of investors and society.

Southwest Airlines, for example, is the iconic company for encouraging its employees to have fun at work. It even goes so far as to differentiate itself through humor in the intensely competitive airline industry. Southwest's former CEO, Herb Kelleher, became famous for the many ways in which he instilled a culture of fun in his company. They included things such as publicly arm-wrestling other CEOs for rights to advertising slogans, dressing up as Elvis Presley or in drag at work, hiding in his plane's overhead bins and surprising his staff, and many other laugh-inducing antics that make work more like play.

Southwest employees have taken humor as serious business and have made it part of their everyday interactions. The following are some examples of Southwest's funny in-flight announcements:

> "Weather at our destination is 50 degrees with some broken clouds but we'll try to have them fixed before we arrive."
>
> "Your seat cushion can be used for flotation; and, in the event of an emergency water landing, please paddle to shore and take them with our compliments."
>
> "As you exit the plane, make sure to gather all of your belongings. Anything left behind will be distributed evenly among the flight attendants. Please do not leave children or spouses."
>
> (After a very hard landing): "That was quite a bump, and I know what y'all are thinking. I'm here to tell you it wasn't the airline's fault, it wasn't the pilot's fault, it wasn't the flight attendant's fault . . . it was the asphalt!"[2]

But it was not just fun and joy at work that Herb Kelleher emphasized among his employees. It was also the recognition of who they were as individuals through the simple act of listening to them well. As a result, he became an inspiration to his employees as well as other executives in the industry. Doug Parker, CEO of US Airways, said of him, "He is so good at listening, and has really taught me how important it is to listen to your employees. If you watch Herb in action, it really is phenomenal. He is completely engaged and never looks over your shoulders to see who else is in the room. It's not out of principle. *It's just who he is*" (emphasis added).[3]

All these efforts at encouraging employees to delight in their work and at recognizing their efforts have paid off handsomely for Southwest. It is the most financially successful of all major US airlines—the only one that had thirty-nine consecutive years of profitability in an industry notorious for bankruptcies and business losses.[4]

Sustained delight introduces a simultaneously broad and deep definition of business success to anchor business leadership. According to this definition, the greater the breadth (across customers, employees, investors, and society) and depth (across the material, human, natural, and Being levels of self) of sustained delight, the more successful the business. In asking the questions outlined above, you may come to think that such sustained delight is an end-state vision that is impossible to achieve. But this is the nature of all end-state visions—they serve as a guiding light (the North Star, or perhaps the star Bhrigu) even if they can never be attained fully.

Long-Term Stakeholder Well-Being

If sustained delight is an end-state vision of success, then what is the compass that Being-centered leaders can use to indicate whether their business is pointing in this direction? The concept of *long-term stakeholder well-being* can be one because it measures the long-term health of an entity, such as a person, business, or nation. As the story of Bhrigu illustrates, the natural state of health of all beings is joy, or sustained delight. For Being-centered leaders, well-being is a natural choice as a compass for sustained delight.

Evaluating corporate success in terms of the long-term well-being of the corporation's stakeholders—rather than through narrow measures such as material profits, shareholder returns, or market value—has strong justification. Similar arguments for measuring a nation's prosperity through national well-being, rather than gross domestic product (GDP), have become very popular.

One reason for the growing disenchantment with GDP is that it measures only material well-being because it is based on material throughput. GDP says nothing about the future prosperity of the nation, and it ignores inequalities in income distribution among a society's members. Also, GDP does not say anything about the nation's prosperity in other forms of capital—human, social, natural, and Being-related.

Finally, GDP views consumption as a yardstick for production, without separating the wasteful and the harmful from the good. For example, the construction of prisons and the waging of wars add to the GDP, which are hardly positive indicators of national well-being.

Conventional measures of business success have similar limitations as GDP: they are directed at material success, are oriented to the short term, focus largely on investors rather than all stakeholders, and disregard other forms of capital that are foundational to material capital (as we saw in chapter 4). These limitations can be addressed by anchoring business success in the long-term well-being of corporate stakeholders, such as employees, customers, investors, and society, and can be described as follows:

$$\text{Business Success} = \sum \text{Long-term well-being of corporate stakeholders}$$

In the above equation, $\sum$ represents the sum over all the key groups of stakeholders. In turn, the well-being of each group is based on the extent to which the business enables the long-term well-being of its material, humanistic, natural, and universal selves.[5]

Interestingly, the Sanskrit word for happiness (*sukha*) is derived from *su* (good) and *kha* (axle-hole). In the agrarian society of ancient India, where the cart was the primary means of transportation, a good axle symbolized happiness. When business leaders unduly emphasize the short term, one group of stakeholders such as investors (or even themselves) over others, or one kind of self or capital (such as material), the axle of business success is unbalanced.

In chapter 1, I showed some evidence why sustainable companies outperform less-sustainable ones in the long term. This is true even if we use conventional financial measures of success such as market value, return on investment, and return on equity. A recent book, *Conscious Capitalism*, by John Mackey (the co-CEO of Whole Foods) and Raj Sisodia (a business-school professor), summarizes other evidence.[6] It concludes that businesses that emphasize the long-term well-being of all their key stakeholders perform financially better than others.

For example, during 1996–2011, whether you used a five-year, ten-year, or fifteen-year timeline, these companies (which the authors call firms of endearment, or FOEs) gave greater returns to their investors than the Standard & Poor's (S&P) 500. This difference increased over time, with the FOEs' fifteen-year return on investment (1,646 percent) being ten times as much as the S&P 500 (157 percent).

In other words, companies that are good to all their stakeholders also make their investors richer. This is because when compared to other companies, their customers like them a lot more, their employees are more engaged and productive, the public is more favorable to them, and their suppliers work better with them. All of this leads to lower marketing, administrative, sales, production, and other costs.

The unique contribution of the business success formula given in this chapter is that it is a systemic way to consider the well-being of different levels of identity or sense of self of all key stakeholders. This way of anchoring business success is similar to contemporary health-care trends that define personal health in terms of the long-term well-being of our *whole* self rather than just our physical body.

As we saw in chapter 4, such long-term well-being of business depends on the extent to which business leaders preserve and renew the balance among key forms of capital (material, human, natural, and Being-related). When they are successful, Being-centered leaders demonstrate the principle of correspondence that is central to the Upanishads: *The long-term well-being of individuals, businesses, and nations is similar because of these groups' shared connections.*

When business success is anchored in this perspective of business success, the gap between a business doing well for itself and for the world reduces.[7] When business leaders internalize this approach, their actions flow *authentically* from it.[8] They can then lead by example by being far more inclusive than other leaders. The lower bird of business leadership can then take confident steps toward the higher bird.

Natura: Stakeholder Well-Being in Practice

Natura Cosméticos, a Brazil-based beauty, personal care, and household products firm, is an outstanding example of the kind of company I am talking about. It is also often ranked among the top five sustainable companies in the world.[9] It's current CEO, Alessandro Carlucci, attributes this success in part to his getting in touch with his feminine side, which has made him a better manager.

As Carlucci said, "Having developed a feminine soul today is not just a pleasure, it's an opportunity. . . . The business world is normally a more rational world, more objective, more straight to the point, and so more masculine. It's not that men are all like that. . . . It's just that we have many women here. The emotional, intuitive, caring side is more present, and so I learned to work in a company where things like that are valued."[10]

Carlucci has deepened the company's already tremendous commitment to nature, even as it delivers material gain to its stakeholders. Natura's commitment extends especially to safeguarding the

Amazon forest from where it derives its ingredients, as well as to the tribes and indigenous population that live within and outside it. For Carlucci, this quest to find the right balance among these different interests begins with asking the right questions.

As he said, "Most important is not to guarantee that we are balanced, but that we are asking ourselves, what are the economic, social and environmental impacts of everything we do? The question is more important than the answer. No one knows the right balance, but we include those things in all initiatives."[11]

In a direct reflection of the kind of business success proposed as an anchor in this book, Carlucci and Natura believe deeply in enhancing the well-being of their stakeholders. He said, "Here at Natura we believe that well-being should be felt and experienced by everybody. . . . We believe that the value and longevity of a company is measured by its ability to promote the sustainable development of society."[12]

He remarked, "What motivates me the most is to see that I'm part of a group of people that wants to do business and, at the same time, contribute to the well-being of people, society and the planet."[13] The company's slogan, printed in large white letters on its São Paulo headquarters' glass walls, is *bem estar bem* (well being/being well), where beauty is about everyone's well-being. Natura sees itself in the business of "aesthetics and ethics," or beauty and truth.

Natura's focus on general well-being has also been good for the material well-being of its stakeholders. The company dominates the Brazilian market for beauty products and deploys over 1.5 million "consultants," mostly female, who directly sell cosmetics and other beauty and hygiene products door to door in Brazil and other Latin American countries.

Natura is also expanding globally in an aggressive way, opening locations in France, the United Kingdom, the United States, and Australia. Natura's global sales in 2011 exceeded $3 billion, which was 9 percent above the previous year. Its share prices have climbed steadily, and its earnings per share outperformed analyst expectations in 2012. Shareholder returns clearly have not suffered, even though they are only part of a broader focus on the well-being of all the company's stakeholders.

In a *Harvard Business Review* cover story on the 100 best CEOs in the world in 2012, Carlucci was in the rarefied 5 percent of trend-setting CEOs who delivered great financial performance while also excelling on social and environmental dimensions. According to the story, Carlucci is "a leader among CEOs who believe that alleviating poverty and inequality and protecting the environment are intimately tied to their business agendas."[14]

The Inner World of a Leader: Dr. V

If the world outside is a reflection of the world inside, then what is the inner world of a Being-centered leader like? To understand it better, consider the story of a business leader hardly known outside his country. It is the story of Dr. Govindappa Venkataswamy (Dr. V to all who knew him), a physician who started the Aravind Eye Care System in India to provide services to the blind and created a business that excelled financially and compassionately.[15]

Since its founding in 1976, Aravind has provided high-quality and highly affordable services to 32 million patients and performed more than 4 million surgeries. Despite the majority of these surgeries being free or heavily subsidized (costing $15 on average), Aravind has a robust business model that generated an operating surplus of $13 million on revenues of $29 million in 2008–9. Aravind's costs of operations were about 1 percent of the costs of comparable services by the UK's National Health Service, which meant that Aravind was actually a $3 billion business that was a hundred times more cost-effective than similar organizations.

When he passed away in 2006 at the age of eighty-eight, Dr. V left behind a thirty-two-hundred-person team that was one of the most efficient, compassionate, and innovative in the world for providing high-quality health services on a large scale. In sheer productivity, Aravind's surgeons are far ahead of others. They average more than two thousand cataract surgeries a year, compared to the Indian average of four hundred and a US average of two hundred. Dr. V himself did more than one hundred thousand surgeries in his life.

But the arc of a Being-centered leader's life is not merely in financial and other material accomplishments. It is also in the connections forged to Being and the world. I describe below how Dr. V made these connections during the four stages of the REAL road map. In doing so, I will quote extensively from Dr. V's journal entries of his efforts to realize Being and the many eyewitness accounts of his work, all captured beautifully by his biographers in the book *Infinite Vision*.

Recognition

For Dr. V, there was a deep *recognition* that his work had a higher purpose. He noted in his journal, "To some of us, bringing divine consciousness to our daily activities is the Goal. The Hospital work gives an opportunity for this spiritual growth. In your own growth you widen your own consciousness and you feel the suffering of others in you." A friend said, "He told me that for him, God existed in the place where all beings were interconnected. He was able to fuse the power of an unsentimental approach to treating poor people in the most effective way, with the moral imagination to see people, really see them, and listen to their needs and dreams."[16]

Dr. V's journals are filled with this recognition of Being, even as he sought the practical. For example, they included entries such as "How to organize and build more hospitals like McDonalds" (reflecting a desire to provide affordable care on a large scale, just as McDonald's provided large-scale affordable food), while Dr. V repeatedly asked, "How do I become a perfect instrument?"[17]

Experience

Such a deep recognition of his higher purpose and relationships was the result of numerous experiences in Dr. V's life—a few of note with Sri Aurobindo and his disciples. Sri Aurobindo was one of India's foremost philosopher-sages of the twentieth century and had reinterpreted the Upanishads in ways that inspired many people throughout the world. His approach was called Integral Yoga and taught that humanity was *collectively* evolving its consciousness toward Being. Moreover, Being could be sought by working actively in this world rather than by renouncing it. Sri Aurobindo's spiritual companion, the Mother, was considered the worldly manifestation of Integral Yoga, and she actively guided their disciples in his teachings.

Dr. V met Sri Aurobindo once at his ashram (resting place) in Pondicherry in southern India in 1950, just before the sage passed away. Dr. V was drawn deeply to Integral Yoga and its combination of the practical and the profound: it was a natural extension of the ethic of hard work that he had absorbed from his father. He felt personally drawn to the Mother and met with her a few times at her ashram.

These few direct experiences with Sri Aurobindo and the Mother had such a profound impact on Dr. V that he named the eye-care hospital he founded Aravind, after the first name of Sri Aurobindo. Dr. V would experience the Mother's presence on several occasions in his life. He recorded one such experience in a journal entry in 1991: "Last night I had a clear indication of Mother's Force entering me. I felt a wide space inside my inner being. I felt deep inside me there was a presence with a small light, just a spark. I felt it must become a fire burning strongly. Felt a good will, feeling of benevolence. I could stand up strongly without being moved by anything."[18]

Anchoring

Through these and many other experiences, Dr. V increased his initial dim recognition of his higher purpose and his relationships to the world around him. He found ways to anchor his fledgling eye-care organization in a definition of success that was radically different from the typical business's. But this anchoring required constant and difficult inner work throughout the next thirty years of Aravind.

Aravind had three unwritten rules: (1) never turn anyone away, (2) never compromise on quality, and (3) be completely self-reliant. They were based on the higher bird of service to everyone rather than on the lower bird of competition and comparison. For more than forty years, Dr. V immersed himself in daily readings of Sri Aurobindo's writings, especially his poem *Savitri*. This poem, one of the longest in the world, is an allegory for the lower bird's efforts to realize the higher bird. Each time he finished the poem, Dr. V would begin all over again. He said, "It is very difficult to understand *Savitri*, just like it is very difficult to realize the soul. But you keep trying, and sometimes you get an inkling of it."[19]

Despite the struggle, the anchoring was also a source of joy. A plaque beneath a portrait of Dr. V in the lobby of one of his medical laboratories captures his words: "Intelligence and capability are not enough. There must be the joy of doing something beautiful."[20] This anchoring was also not just about business principles of high volume, high quality, affordability, and sustainability, all of which were important to Aravind's definition of business success. Much more so, it was about reaching people in a human way. Anchoring in the higher consciousness of Being changes one's whole approach to work.

Leadership by Example

One way in which Dr. V led by example was by helping others see surgery not as a procedure but as a key step in a larger chain of connection involving the life of the patient. As his biographers noted, he helped others see that "when a doctor restores sight to a woman who is able to work in the fields again, her child has a better chance of going to school and then a better shot at finding a job that will break the cycle of poverty their family has lived in for generations. When a doctor, working with a team, gives sight to not just one or ten but a thousand or tens of thousands of such men and women, then not one family but an entire village, district, state, eventually perhaps an entire country will, in a small but significant way, be helped toward a better future."[21]

Through Dr. V's efforts, doctors and nurses at Aravind saw the patient as a *human being*, rather than as an individual paying lucrative fees. One team member recalled, "Dr. V always told us we shouldn't have high charges. 'Think of every patient who comes in as your aunt or your grandmother from the village,' he would say. 'Then automatically compassion will come. Once that feeling comes, then you'll naturally do a good job.'"[22] This attention to patient well-being had a big influence on the founding team members. While they were cost-conscious individually, they were not focused on business profits. Despite this lack of direct focus on profits, Dr. V and his colleagues managed to create a business with healthy operating profits of 45 percent.

Dr. V's unusual insights could transform the lives of the people around him. A US-based surgeon named William Stewart was inspired to change his calling because of Dr. V. He had visited Aravind to learn more about the organization's reconstructive surgery after an eye operation. When he returned to the United States, he received a letter from Dr. V, who had seen something in him: "I see your work evolving from a one-to-one practice to being more about consciousness and larger groups of people."[23] Stewart would subsequently leave surgical practice and set up an institute to promote integrative medicine by combining the best practices of the East and the West. He recalled, "Dr. V and Aravind changed my perspective. It was at Aravind that I saw that health and healing are not just scientific but also spiritual pursuits."[24]

A Vale of Becoming

The life and legacy of Dr. V is a great example of how Being-centered leaders cultivate a fine balance of shared purpose and material profits that enables their businesses to succeed, even in the face of overwhelming odds. Underlying Aravind's success was Dr. V's constant striving to become a more perfect being, which he called becoming "an instrument of a higher purpose."

When I see these extraordinary struggles to become a more perfect being, I am reminded of a verse from the Isha Upanishad: "O Being, remember these struggles, remember!" These struggles accompany all meaningful journeys of Being-centered leadership and are integral to the courageous work the lower bird has to do to reach the higher bird. Dr. V's strivings also remind me of the philosopher Krishna Chaitanya's remarks on Mahatma Gandhi: "Gandhiji himself could have stated the meaning of his life and death very simply: this life, this earth, is a vale of soul-making."[25]

Whether we call it soul, foundational principle, ultimate reality, or Being, this is the core of Being-centered leadership: *this life, this world, is a great valley of Being's becoming for business leaders.*

TWEETS

- Sustained delight introduces a simultaneously broad and deep definition of business success to anchor business leadership.

- Business Success = $\sum$ Long-term well-being of corporate stakeholders.

- The long-term well-being of individuals, businesses, and nations are similar because of the groups' shared connections.

- "Intelligence and capability are not enough. There must be the joy of doing something beautiful."—Dr. V.

- This life, this world, is a great valley of Being's becoming for business leaders.

SEEDS

- What does *joy* or *sustained delight* in your workplace truly mean?

- What are the top three changes that would happen to your company's way of functioning if it anchored itself in long-term stakeholder well-being?

- What are the ways in which your shareholders would benefit from implementing this new definition of business success in your company?

- How do Alessandro Carlucci's lessons on well-being translate to your company?

- How do the lessons from Dr. V's quest for becoming a more perfect instrument translate to your own work? How do you relate to such a striving?

PART 5

Leading by Example

The one who knows the best and the great,
Becomes the best and the great.
The one who knows the foundation,
Stands firm in the world.
The one who knows that which gives shelter,
Becomes a shelter for others.

CHĀNDOGYA UPANISHAD

9

Leading by Inclusion

Know the Self as the chariot's lord,
Our body as the chariot itself,
Know the rider as our intelligence,
Our mind is the rider's reins,
Our physical senses are the horses, they say,
While material objects are the paths they travel.
He who is without understanding,
With unrestrained mind and senses out of control,
Is like a chariot out of balance, with bad horses.
KAṬHA UPANISHAD

O nce it has found a steady anchor and is less affected by the storm, the lower bird can begin to take the confident steps that will lead it to the higher bird. It now has different paths by which it can scale the tree and lead the way for the other birds in the lower branches. One way for Being-centered business leaders to lead by example is to be inclusive and show commitment to the material and humanistic well-being of stakeholders *besides* investors and themselves.

The problem with existing ways of defining business success is not that they include material well-being. The problem is that they are *unbalanced* because they focus overwhelmingly on material well-being or focus on a small set of stakeholders (for example, the investors and senior management) to the exclusion of others. Here's a story from the Chāndogya Upanishad on the dangers of such a focus.[1]

Gods and Demons

Once long ago, it became known to the gods and demons that Prajāpati, the Lord of Beings, knew the secret to discovering the timeless being that is the universal self and the great power that it conferred.[2] Prajāpati was known to have said, "When this self is perceived and known, all the worlds are known, and all our desires are satisfied." The gods conferred among themselves and appointed Indra to approach Prajāpati and seek this knowledge. Among the demons, Virochana was given this difficult task.

And so Indra and Virochana together sought out Prajāpati with an offering of firewood in their hands and lived with him and served him for thirty-two years. Then Prajāpati asked them, "Why have you lived with me for thirty-two years? What is it that you seek to know from me?"

They told him what they had heard, "Sir, people report that you have said, 'The self that is free from old age, death, sorrow, from hunger and thirst, and from all evils—that is the self that should be discovered. When this self is known, all the worlds are known and all the desires are satisfied.' Sir, teach us about this self."

Then Prajāpati told them, "Gaze at yourselves in a pan of water. What do you see?"

They told him, "Sir, we see a perfect likeness of ourselves, down to the hairs on our body and our fingernails."

The Lord of Beings replied, "Now decorate yourself beautifully, dress well, and then look again in a pail of water. What do you see?"

They replied, "Sir, just as we are beautifully decorated and well-dressed, so too are these that we see in the water."

Prajāpati said, "That is the self, the immortal that is free from all fear."

Virochana and Indra left with their hearts filled with gladness for they thought they knew the self. When Prajāpati saw them depart with contentment, he said to himself, "There they go, the two of them, without truly learning about and discovering the self. The one that remains deceived by this connection, whether god or demon, will soon be defeated."

Virochana, much thrilled with his newfound knowledge, returned to his fellow demons and exulted, "It is this body that we should praise and worship in this world. It is this body we should care for. When someone praises and extols this body alone, he will win this world and the next." But Indra, chief of the gods, saw the danger from this knowledge even before he had returned to the gods.

Unsatisfied, Indra retraced his steps and returned to Prajāpati, once again with offerings of firewood in his hands. On seeing him, Prajāpati asked, "My dear Indra, did you not leave with contentment in your heart at receiving my knowledge? Why have you come back disappointed?"

Indra replied, "If this is the self as you say, well-decorated and beautiful when the body is well-decorated and beautiful, then this self too will be blind and crippled when this body becomes blind and crippled. This self too will die when this body dies. I see nothing useful in this knowledge of the self."

Prajāpati responded happily, "Indra, it is as you say. You have seen through this knowledge that I gave you. Stay with me and learn from me for another thirty-two years and I will reveal the secret knowledge of the self."

But twice more did the Lord of Beings try to fool Indra, once with the hidden connection of the self to the person who goes happily forth in a dream and then again to the one who is fast asleep and free from dreams, serene and calm. But each time, Indra left with new knowledge and returned again to Prajāpati, having seen through these unsatisfying connections. For dreams can be fearful and deep sleep makes us unaware of ourselves.

Then at last, Prajāpati instructed Indra to stay with him and prepare for another five years. After these one hundred one long years of preparation, Prajāpati revealed to Indra the real nature of the timeless being behind our thoughts and our mind: "This very self rejoices as it perceives with his mind, with that divine sight, these objects of desire found in the world. . . . When someone discovers this self and comes to perceive it, he will obtain all the worlds and have all his desires fulfilled."[3]

For Virochana and the demons, the self could be realized only through external ornamentation. For Indra and the gods, this knowledge was not enough. Instead, self-knowledge came from recognizing the being behind our thinking, seeing, and feeling faculties. This was Ātman, the Being that they were seeking.

When Prajāpati cautioned about the connections that deceive us, he was referring to the problems of materialism, which may be defined as an excessive and unbalanced emphasis on making money and having possessions. People who emphasize material values in an unbalanced way often suffer from low personal self-esteem and well-being.[4] This is because materialism is a symptom of a deeper inability to meet one's core psychological needs for safety and sustenance.

Materialism intensifies this suffering by putting people on a "hedonic treadmill" where satisfying their need for self-esteem and competence is always just beyond reach. As was the case with Gopal from my class in business school, it can deepen people's isolation by impeding their ability to form meaningful relationships and have a sense of personal freedom and authenticity in their lives. In brief, materialism leads to an unhealthy sense of self.

Stepping off the Treadmill: The Inclusive Materialist

What is true of the personal self is also true of the business self. Business leaders who emphasize the pursuit of profits and other material values excessively will damage the overall well-being of the corporation. The most common way this manifests itself is business leaders' emphasis on financial returns to shareholders as *the* measure of business well-being. Here, business performance becomes defined exclusively in terms of profits, market capitalization, and other financial criteria that benefit shareholders. In this type of environment, customers and other stakeholders can easily fall from the forefront of business decision making.

The great danger in materialism that defines success narrowly in terms of profits is that many investors see a corporation as a means for maximizing their *short-term* financial returns. Free-market capitalism that encourages such short-term behavior is the treadmill within which anxious business leaders perpetually chase investor needs that are insatiable over time. Although one benefit of trying to please short-term investors is that they efficiently allocate market resources among existing opportunities, its chief drawback is what Prajāpati drew attention to: equating material wealth to the needs of the self is not the means to genuine well-being.

One way in which business leaders can begin to step off the treadmill of materialism is by emphasizing *long-term* financial returns to investors. At first glance, this may appear impossible. After all, what is a business leader to do when the company's investors focus on short-term returns? Would this not be like tilting at windmills, given what happened to PepsiCo's Nooyi, as described in chapter 7? But the contrasting behaviors of Indra and Virochana in response to Prajāpati's material inducement suggest otherwise. Both Virochana and Indra had a choice when it came to accepting Prajāpati's offer of wisdom. Virochana chose to accept it without questioning it, while Indra saw through to the hidden dangers of such wisdom.

The lesson for business leaders is clear. By arguing that investors are responsible for the leader's own short-term behavior, they have chosen to accept conventional wisdom without questioning it. The reality is that short-term behavior by investors is often encouraged by the behavior of business leaders themselves.

Don't just take my word for it. Researchers have studied the terms used in the transcripts of more than seventy thousand quarterly conference calls on earnings made by over thirty-six hundred firms during

2002–8.[5] Their conclusion: business leaders that are short-term oriented attract investors who fixate on quarterly numbers. When it comes to short-termism, it seems that it takes two to tango.

In his book *Saving Capitalism from Short-Termism*, business scholar Alfred Rappaport gives a fascinating treatment of the origins and effects of the short-term orientation that dominates business.[6] One main cause is that corporate investors have not adapted their compensation practices to encourage long-term thinking among corporate leaders who spend other people's money.

The other main cause is the flip side: corporate leaders are in thrall to providing quarterly earnings guidance and meeting investors' quarterly earnings expectations, as well as the tyranny of the short-term share price. The message is clear: if this dysfunctional tango is to break up, one of the partners has to refuse to dance to the tune of short-termism.

There is strong evidence that the companies that dance to a longer tune will create significantly greater long-term shareholder value than those that do not.[7] Business leaders need more inspiration and courage, not more evidence, to commit to long-term value creation. This could mean refusing to give quarterly earnings guidance to investors, as many have suggested. To do so requires a change in the mind-sets and beliefs of business leaders, which is the refrain of this book.

Whatever the approach chosen, true leadership swims against the current of conventional thinking and settles on the shores of a different wisdom. If it were not difficult to do so, it would not have been called *leadership*. The actions of Colman Mockler, former CEO of Gillette, suggest that it can be done.

In the face of a hostile takeover bid from Revlon that would have delivered an immediate $2.3 billion gain on Gillette's stock (a 44 percent increase), Mockler stuck to his long-term vision for the company. In resisting the takeover, Mockler demonstrated an ability to look beyond short-term gains, staking Gillette's future on radically new technologies that led to the hugely successful Sensor and the Mach3 razors. As a review showed,

If a shareflipper had accepted the 44 percent price premium offered by Ronald Perelman [of Revlon] on October 31, 1986, and then invested the full amount in the general market for ten years, through the end of 1996, he would have come out three times *worse* off than a shareholder who had stayed with Mockler and Gillette. Indeed, the company, its customers, *and* the shareholders would have been ill served had Mockler capitulated to the raiders, pocketed his millions, and retired to a life of leisure.[8]

Another way to step off the treadmill is to improve the material well-being of stakeholders *besides* investors. Employees are the first set of stakeholders to turn to for spreading material wealth. Many business leaders don't truly recognize that better pay and benefits are cost-effective because they reduce turnover costs, as well as lead to more loyal, productive, and engaged employees. But others do.

Take Costco, for example.[9] This large chain in the margin-thin retail industry pays particular attention to its employees' material well-being simply because it is good for business. The company's cofounder, Jim Sinegal, was a protégé of Sol Price, who founded Price Club.

Costco's business and philosophy are based on Sol Price's business model of selling a limited number of items, keeping costs down by relying on customers to buy in bulk, and paying workers well so that they are more productive. Costco's code of ethics puts its customers, employees, and suppliers ahead of its shareholders. Its employees make between 40 and 70 percent more than their major competition (including Wal-Mart and its subsidiary, Sam's Club) and have much better benefits.

Costco's generosity pays off in terms of better corporate performance through lower employee turnover after the first year (6 percent versus Wal-Mart's 44 percent and Sam's Club's 21 percent), reduced recruiting and training costs, and a more efficient and productive workforce that creates better relationships with its customers.

All these corporate benefits lead to a higher profit per employee for Costco when compared to its competition. Despite putting employees ahead of investors, the latter have done very well indeed—Costco's returns to shareholders in the past decade have been twice that of the S&P 500 index and 3.5 times that of Wal-Mart, its chief rival.[10]

The case of Father Arizmendi of the Basque region of Spain is equally compelling.[11] He combined the social teachings of his Catholic faith with an economic vision of solidarity and participation to help the small Basque town of Mondragon recover from economic turmoil after the Spanish Civil War. In 1943, Father Arizmendi started a technical college as a training ground for managers, engineers, and skilled laborers committed to working together cooperatively.

In 1955, Father Arizmendi selected five workers from the Unión Cerrajera company to form Talleres Ulgor (today Fagor Electrodomésticos). Other companies were formed within the Mondragon Cooperative in the decades following. They received support from Caja Laboral, the cooperative credit union founded in 1959 as part of Mondragon.

Today, workers at the lower wage levels of Mondragon make roughly 13 percent more than their counterparts in other companies, while managers at Mondragon earn 30 percent or less comparatively. Mondragon's business success is now a global model for how cooperative capitalism can work in practice, all emanating from the example set by a priest who combined spirituality with business to promote employment in a remote Basque town seventy years ago.

However, corporate well-being extends well beyond the pursuit of material well-being for all stakeholders. If material success is only one foundation for corporate well-being, then how can leaders lead by example on the others?

The Humanist

Another way for Being-centered leaders to lead is to include other levels of identity or personal self by going beyond material well-being and seeking the *humanistic* well-being of their stakeholders. This means nurturing the human and social connections of employees and other stakeholders with one another and the corporation, thereby transforming corporate culture itself.

But this journey requires us to understand who we ourselves are, as the Upanishads emphasize. The life of Ursula Burns, the CEO of Xerox and the only female black CEO of a Fortune 500 company, illustrates why it is the key to becoming a Being-centered leader by example. It is this understanding that connects us to the common humanity that we share with others.

Ursula Burns grew up as a poor black child in the Lower East Side of New York. Her mother washed and ironed clothes for a living and exchanged cleaning services with a local doctor to provide health care for her three children.

Despite these conditions, Ursula learned a valuable lesson from her mother:

> If you just look at the demographics—I was a poor black woman in a poor black family—you would think there was no way in the world that there would be options available to me. The reality is that, despite that, I had very few limitations when I was growing up. I was raised by my mother, who was extremely poor, in a very poor neighbourhood, basically a ghetto.
>
> My mother told me very early in life—and my brother and sister as well—that where we were was not who we were. Where you live, she pointed out, has nothing to do with who you are. Who you are is about your character, it's about the amount of energy you put into things, it's about how much control you take of your whole life. She really believed that you control your destiny, your future.[12]

Another key lesson she learned from her mother was the value of education:

When I was a kid, she couldn't change where we lived; but she could invest a disproportionate amount of her energy and her resources towards our education. . . . My mother's highest pay, ever, was $4,400 a year; yet, somehow she managed to send me to a high school that cost $65 a month. Multiply that by three and you realize that half of her salary went to our education.[13]

This emphasis on education led Burns eventually to a master's degree in mechanical engineering at Columbia University. She joined Xerox in 1981 and has stayed there ever since. Her hard work, dedication, and intelligence soon got noticed. In 1991, she became the executive assistant to the CEO of Xerox. In 2000, she became a senior vice president and began to work closely with Anne Mulcahy, who would later become CEO. In 2009, Burns became CEO, the first time that a Fortune 500 company had a woman-to-woman CEO transition.

Despite these rare accomplishments, Ursula Burns has managed to retain an authenticity, directness, and sense of self-understanding that is remarkable. An emphasis on being authentic and bringing your whole self to the workplace is important for her. She has developed a reputation at Xerox for her directness and her encouragement of employees to be more frank and impatient (and even cranky!) with one another. She said:

Crankiness is a human attribute that when people walk in the door of Xerox, they remain human. So they bring all of the goods, the bads and the uglies to work, and I like all of those things because I think we spend a lot of time here—wherever here is, here it could be anywhere, at home—but around this set of things that we do that we call work. We spend a lot of energy and a lot of time in it and I think that the best way to get the best out of people is to not force them to be something other than they naturally are.[14]

It is still too early to tell whether Ursula Burns's leadership style will bring a successful turnaround at Xerox. From its record high price of $64 per share in 1999, the stock price in early 2013 was only around $9. But Xerox seems to be recovering gradually as its earnings improve and the services division becomes a larger share (now at 52 percent) of the company's sales.

If this turnaround is successful, it will be one of the great stories of corporate America, where a household name that invented an industry (copiers) managed to transition to a whole new set of offerings. Whether or not Burns will be the one ensuring this turnaround, she has already led a unique life of a leader as humanist.

Another great example of a CEO who has tapped into and drawn deeply from this humanism, both for himself and for his employees, is Chip Conley. He is the founder and former CEO of Joie de Vivre Hotels, a boutique hotel chain in Northern California. In 2008—the year in which the economic downturn shut down many businesses—Conley experienced a perfect storm of economic, physical, and psychological crises.[15] The hotel business was severely affected because travel is a discretionary expense that gets readily curtailed when times are tough.

As his company struggled to survive, Conley broke his ankle playing baseball. He contracted a serious infection from ground fertilizer that had gotten into a cut in his leg and was at real risk of having his leg amputated. A short while afterward, while preparing to give a speech, he collapsed from a severe allergic reaction to the antibiotics he was taking to fight the infection. He flatlined while being rushed to the hospital in an ambulance and, in his words, was "dying for about ninety minutes."

In the hospital, after recovering from this near-death experience, Conley returned to a book he had read previously, Viktor E. Frankl's *Man's Search for Meaning*. He recalls thinking, "I've got to figure out how to understand the code in this book and I need to integrate it into my life. And it was at that moment in my hospital room that I decided to turn *Man's Search for Meaning* into an equation." He came up with the "emotional" equation Despair = Suffering – Meaning.

From his study and practice of Buddhism, Conley recognized that suffering is constant while meaning depends on the individual. This set him on a new course of action, what he refers to as a kind of "emotional boot camp." He composed a list each week of emotions he'd been feeling, such as humility, vulnerability, and authenticity, and asked himself, "How am I going to use these emotions next week?"

Some days later, when asked to give a speech to cheer up employees at the struggling Santa Cruz Dream Inn (a hotel owned by Joie de Vivre), Conley decided instead to openly discuss his new equation of despair, suffering, and meaning and the personal struggles he was going through.

When corporations go through a crisis, Conley concluded, leaders should help employees experience an emotional catharsis and give them a sense that they're in it together. In particular, CEOs are also the chief *emotion* officers of their companies, helping their employees deal with their inner conflicts and emotions regarding their work and life.

To further his understanding of happiness, Conley traveled to Bhutan, the Himalayan country famous for measuring success in terms of the happiness of its people. He recognized that the fastest way to feel happy when you're unhappy is to express gratitude—*to want what you already have*. As a result, Conley began engaging in "gratitude practice," where he expressed his gratitude actively and sincerely to someone two to three times a day over the phone or in person.

Conley also came to recognize that the most contagious emotion in a company was anxiety. As he delved further into the matter, he realized that anxiety had two main dimensions: what you don't know and what you can't control. For Conley, this process of self-discovery has taken him out of his company and into the world beyond business's boundaries to explore the relationship between happiness and being. What an eventful journey it has been!

A deep sense of human connection helps when responding to humanitarian crises engendered by corporations. When corporate leaders are detached from this sense of connection, their response to a crisis can be viewed as especially insensitive. The comments made by oil giant BP's CEO, Tony Hayward ("I'm sorry. We're sorry for the massive disruption it's caused their lives. There's no one who wants this over more than I do. I'd like my life back."), that followed the disastrous Deepwater Horizon oil spill in the Gulf of Mexico in 2010 created a public backlash that deeply damaged BP's image.

By contrast, the response of the late James Burke, CEO of the US-based company Johnson & Johnson in 1976–89, to the famous Tylenol crisis of 1982 has become a textbook case of how to lead as a humanist during a corporate crisis involving customers.

When cyanide-laced Tylenol capsules killed seven people in the Chicago area that year, Burke responded immediately and massively to the public scare that followed. He ordered all 32 million Tylenol bottles off the shelves of stores everywhere, even though Tylenol was one of J&J's top-selling products and it would cost $100 million to do so.

He also went on the investigative television show *60 Minutes* to explain his response. But his strategy of hiding nothing from the public was at odds with conventional wisdom. He recalled:

> My son said an interesting thing. He said that I had a philosophy of life which I felt strongly about, and all of a sudden, through an accident, that philosophy was tested, and all my experience was utilized in a unique way. . . . When I decided to go on *60 Minutes*, the head of public relations told me it was the worst decision anyone in this corporation had ever made, and anyone who would risk this corporation that way was totally irresponsible, and he walked out and slammed the door.[16]

This strategy of responding genuinely and transparently to a human crisis worked on multiple levels. Research showed that customers who saw the *60 Minutes* episode were five times more likely to buy J&J's products than those who did not. For the next three months, J&J worked on developing a tamper-resistant bottle to package Tylenol while the product remained unsold.

Once Tylenol was reintroduced into the market, it stormed back within a year to recapture the 35 percent market share it had held previously.[17] The use of tamper-resistant packaging has since become widespread in the industry. After his retirement in 1989, James Burke went on to spearhead efforts to reduce illegal drug use in America. He received the Presidential Medal of Freedom in 2000 for his corporate and civic leadership.

Such humanism can also extend beyond employees and current customers and touch others in society, especially those who are disadvantaged. A great example of a business leader taking the humanistic needs of society as seriously as the materialistic needs of corporations is Danish-born Lars Rebien Sørensen, CEO of Novo Nordisk, Denmark, which provides pharmaceutical products and services for patients with diabetes. Shortly after becoming CEO in 2000, Sørensen set out on an educational world tour, meeting with employees and stakeholders.[18]

In country after country, stakeholders challenged him to play a role that went well beyond business as usual. As he says, "We were directed to a new kind of social leadership—one that would demand that we redefine our goals and rethink our basic mission as a profit-making organization. It was clear that 'the bottom line' could no longer be seen in purely financial terms and that corporate social responsibility would need to go beyond compliance and philanthropy."[19]

Sørensen returned from the trip with a "a sense of direction, convinced that in an unjust and unfair world we could simply no longer retain our 'neutrality.' We had to take side with our customers—people with diabetes. Both those that can pay and those that can't!"[20]

He also believes that access to essential medicine is a fundamental human right and has set as a goal for his company to sell insulin to thirty-three of the world's poorest countries at a price that is less than one-fifth that in more developed countries.

Under his leadership, the company outperformed its competition in how it treated its employees. For example, the ratio of CEO pay to the average pay of employees is 15:1 versus a pharmaceutical average of 93:1. For this excellence across several dimensions, Novo Nordisk was ranked number one in the world in the reputed Corporate Knights 2012 rankings of responsible companies.

We can see some common themes in these examples of CEOs as humanists: genuine contact with other human beings or their own humanness leads to a *recognition* of a greater humanity that underlies their work. This recognition is then *experienced* in ways that are unique to them. They then take the next step that many other leaders fail to do: they persist and find ways to *anchor* themselves in this recognition and experience that changes their attitudes and sense of self. When these changes happen, they truly become leaders who *lead by example* by embodying this humanism in their own lives.

But what happens when this sense of connection extends beyond other human beings and reaches out to other living beings that share our world—and even to the nonliving environment? What happens when it reaches out to touch *future* generations of living beings? We explore next the natural branches that connect the two birds in the tree of business life.

TWEETS

- Existing approaches to success are unbalanced due to their overwhelming focus on the material well-being of shareholders.

- It takes two to tango: business leaders that are short-term oriented attract investors who fixate on quarterly numbers.

- True business leadership swims against the current of conventional thinking and settles on the shores of a different wisdom.

- CEOs are also chief emotion officers, helping employees deal with their inner conflicts and emotions regarding their work and life.

- A leader-humanist seeks the humanistic well-being of stakeholders by nurturing the company's human and social connections to them.

SEEDS

- Describe a decision you were involved in that was driven by meeting the quarterly expectations of analysts. What would you do differently from a long-term perspective and why?

- What would happen at your work if employees brought "all of the goods, the bads, and the uglies" so they can *be* themselves, as Ursula Burns wanted?

- What would happen if you or your CEO were like Chip Conley and were open about your struggles at work?

- What new kind of "social leadership" could you or your CEO undertake, as Lars Rebien Sørensen did? How would it make you more effective?

10

Leading as a Steward

This whole world is covered by the Self,
Whether moving or still:
Support yourself by renouncing ownership,
Set not your heart on wealth that is not yours.
ISHA UPANISHAD

The lower bird has an alternative to the humanistic branches that connect it to the higher bird: nature's own branches also lead to the top of the tree. For business leadership, the core of this alternative is *stewardship*, the concept that business and humanity are guardians, rather than pillaging owners, of nature and its elements. As stewards, the role of business leaders is to preserve and renew nature for future generations of human and other living beings rather than dominate nature for their own purposes. If business leaders are stewards, then who is the real owner?

The True Owner

The Upanishads have a ready answer: it is the universal self (Ātman), which interpenetrates this world but is beyond it. In the Chāndogya Upanishad, a homeless person named Raikva tells Jānaśruti, the richest man of the town, a tale that illustrates who the true owner of this world is.[1] One day, while two learned men were eating, a student came up to them and asked for food. When the men turned him away, the student said, "Who is that being who guards this world and to whom all this wealth truly belongs? Though unseen by all, he is present everywhere."

145

One of the men reflected on this question and then replied thoughtfully, "This being is the Ātman, the true devourer of this world whose greatness is beyond measure. He is the one we worship." The man then turned to his companion and said, "Let us share our food with this student." After narrating this story, Raikva told Jānaśruti, "All this truly belongs to the Ātman, the great being that has grasped this whole world with his teeth. The one who knows this truth can sink his teeth too into this world and become ever nourished."

Mahatma Gandhi, who possessed less than ten things at his death (including sandals, an eating bowl, a watch, and spectacles), is one of the best exemplars of the stewardship principle of supporting oneself through renouncing ownership. He thought that the third line ("Support yourself by renouncing ownership") given in the verse above ought to be considered one of the great sayings of the Upanishads. He went even further and said that if the Upanishads were to be lost suddenly, their core meaning could be reconstructed fully from this first verse of the Isha Upanishad.

At the heart of the stewardship concept is the emphasis on long-term outcomes that go beyond one's own lifetime and pleasures. As stewards, we preserve and renew nature and its resources for the living beings that come after us. They are not just for our own pleasure because of the simple reason that we are not their true owners.

Ray Anderson: America's "Greenest CEO"

Consider the remarkable story of the late Ray Anderson, founder and former CEO of Interface, a billion-dollar US-based carpeting company that he started in 1973 after a trip to Europe where he discovered modular or "tile" carpeting. He was the first major American CEO to have come out strongly for protecting nature, pursuing it with a passion and pragmatism that made him a hero to many. He was often called the *greenest CEO in America* during his lifetime. However, for the first twenty years of the company's existence, he was mainly concerned with making profits and implementing a business model that was radically new to the industry. Everything changed in 1994.

Anderson was trying to come up with a sustainability vision for his company that year and all he could think of was to comply with the many rules and regulations that the government produced. But he happened to read Paul Hawken's *Ecology of Commerce*, which had just come across his desk. He said that the experience was "an epiphany, a rude awakening, an eye-opening experience, and the point of the story felt just like the point of a spear driven straight into my heart."[2]

Anderson felt he was "convicted as a plunderer of the Earth."[3] Business's impacts on nature, particularly due to its dependence on fossil fuels, felt to him like "the theft of our children's future" ("tomorrow's child," as he said) that would someday be considered a crime.[4] He resolved to make his company fully sustainable and set the then-unprecedented goal of zero impact on nature by 2020. He pursued this goal ("Mission Zero") with tremendous focus, reaching 60 percent of it when he died of liver cancer in 2011.

Ray Anderson continues to inspire the people in his company, and their memorial to him is touching and simple in its genuineness.[5] They were inspired by his vision of changing the world and by his humility as a person. His successor recalled in an interview, "He always put the company and the people ahead of himself. Always."[6] He was very clear that sustainability was good for business. It helped Interface cut $400 million in waste and double profits.

He said in a moving TED Talk in 2009, "I always make the business case for sustainability. It's so compelling. Our costs are down, not up. . . . Our products are the best they've ever been. . . . Our people are galvanized around a shared higher purpose . . . and the goodwill in the marketplace. . . . We might not have survived the recession without the advantages of sustainability." He concluded, "We are each and everyone a part of the web of life. . . . We have a choice to make during our brief visit to this beautiful blue and green living planet: to hurt it or to help it."[7] Although no longer in this world, he continues to top many people's list of CEOs as stewards.

Eileen Fisher: Stewardship and Well-Being

A number of CEOs have taken a deep interest in stewardship, including well-known business leaders such as Yvon Chouinard of Patagonia, former CEO Lee Scott of Wal-Mart, Jeff Immelt of GE, John Mackey of Whole Foods, and others. Here, I want to describe the experiences of Eileen Fisher, of the eponymous women's clothing company. She is less known globally but well recognized in her own industry for the simplicity and durability of her designs.

While stewardship is about many things, simplicity and durability are two of its key principles that Fisher has made a centerpiece of her many years in the industry. High-end designs are typically not associated with environmental stewardship, which makes Fisher all the more interesting, as is the way in which holistic well-being is woven into all aspects of her business.[8]

Because simple and durable designs are central to her style, the company's sustainability efforts flow authentically from its approach to design. Not only are the clothes meant to last long, but they also use a lot of natural fibers that are eco-friendly. Specialty fabrics dominate her business, and silk blends are popular, which makes using organic materials expensive and difficult. Nevertheless, she uses organic cotton for most of her cotton needs and has switched to fabrics that are less energy intensive during customer use. For example, 90 percent of her spring 2012 line of clothes was cold-water washable.

Hers became the first American fashion company to work with *bluesign*, a Swiss-developed standard for safe and sustainable manufacturing of textiles, chemicals, and other products. This emphasis on stewardship extends to the company's warehouses (which are outfitted with solar panels), headquarters (which has won architectural awards for being nature focused), support for wind farms, encouragement of sustainable practices among suppliers in Peru and elsewhere, and encouragement of customers to recycle their used clothes by taking them back through the Green Eileen program. Stewardship pervades the entire company.

This uniqueness has led to considerable recognition for her company in the typically nature-unfriendly world of women's clothing. What is especially interesting about the company is that stewardship is a means to enable the company's purpose of stakeholder well-being, delight, and connection. In my own consulting with Fortune 500 companies, I have found that the key to corporate stewardship is not to focus on it for its own sake but to *connect it to something that the company has deeply cared about all its life.*

In Fisher's case, stewardship is directly connected to the company's mission, which is to enable individual growth and well-being that nourish the mind, body, and spirit; create a joyful work atmosphere; and promote social consciousness that includes humanity and nature.

For Fisher, these are not just empty promises but everyday practices that make her company very different from its competition. She refuses to brand her name or logo on her line of clothes because she wants the clothes to be about them and not herself. The company does not put on supermodel-based runway shows, unlike most other fashion houses. Her employees begin the day with yoga and other centering practices, and everyone gets a $1,000 per year "wellness allowance."

At the same time, the privately held company has been very successful financially. In 2012, it employed more than 1,000 people, made sales in excess of $300 million, had over sixty store locations, and was expanding into Canada and England. But this financial success is a result of focusing on what matters at the core rather than on the bottom line for its own sake. As Fisher said,

> You know, if you're paying attention to what you care about and what you love—and for me, how the whole thing comes

together—then it tends to work at the bottom line. . . . Bottom line is really just numbers that reflect what's happening in the center. And so you pay attention to what's happening in the center, and when that's right, the numbers follow.[9]

The common theme in the lives of Ray Anderson and Eileen Fisher is a focus on what has given them deep and lasting, rather than temporary, satisfaction. This long-term persistence has made them realize the importance of stewardship over nature rather than nature's rapid depletion for short-term gain.

Chasing Pleasure, Seeking Joy

Pursuit of long-term outcomes gives real joy, while short-term pursuits give passing pleasure. Pleasure itself is the satisfaction of a desire. Satisfying the desire does not lead to human growth but urges us on to ever newer and more exciting pleasures. In essence, pleasure has to do with gratifying our wants, and since our wants are limitless, the desire for pleasure is never satisfied. Joy, on the other hand, is the experience of expressing our essential human faculties. Joy has to do with recognizing and meeting our needs, which are limited and essential. Unlike pleasures, the experience of joy stays with us.

It is much easier to choose the pleasurable (short-term path) over what is good (long-term path), and this is likely why business leaders find it difficult to become stewards. While the latter path is hard to tread, like a razor's edge, according to the Upanishads, it is also the path that the wise follow. The true leader is one who chooses this path, as the god of Death tells Nachiketas in the Katha Upanishad.[10] For many people I know, their favorite story in all the Upanishads is the one about Nachiketas.

Once long ago, Uśan, the son of the sage Vājaśravas, decided to give away all his possessions in a great sacrifice; but the cattle he gave away had already been milked dry, nor could they bear any more calves. Nachiketas, the young son of Uśan, observed what was happening and thought, "What use is a sacrifice when that which is given away is of no use to anyone? My father will surely go to the lands of the joyless after his death if he gives away such useless gifts."

The thought came to Nachiketas that he should offer himself as sacrifice so that Uśan could be spared this fate. And so he asked, "Father, to whom will you give me in sacrifice?" Uśan, absorbed in his rituals, did not pay attention to his son.

Twice more did Nachiketas ask to be given away. Uśan finally grew irritated with his interruptions and said in anger and without thought, "I'll give you to Death!" Once the curse had been uttered, it could not be taken back.

And so Nachiketas made his way to the abode of Yama, the god of Death. Death was away on some other business, and Nachiketas had to wait without food and water for three nights. When Death returned home, a voice called out to him in warning, "Beware of this sacred guest who stayed in your house for three nights without food and water. Appease him, or else lose all that you own."

Death said hastily, and with alarm, to Nachiketas, "You came as a guest to my home, and you spent three nights without my hospitality. I offer three boons to you in homage so that I may be spared misfortune from insulting a sacred guest."

Nachiketas' first boon was that his father's anger be appeased and that he be welcomed with joy when he returned to the land of the living. When Death readily gave him this wish, Nachiketas then asked for his second boon: "You, O Death, know well the sacred fire and fire altar that leads from earth to heaven. Explain them to me." Death then instructed Nachiketas on the fire of creation, the origin of the world, the types and number of bricks to use in creating the fire altar, and how these bricks should be arranged.

When Nachiketas repeated these instructions clearly, Death was very pleased and gave him another boon, "This fire of sacrifice will be named after you, O Nachiketas. Whoever performs the fire sacrifice of Nachiketas will pass beyond life and death, beyond sorrows, and attain peace in heaven. And now, what do you choose for your third boon, Nachiketas?"

Now at last, Nachiketas asked, "At a man's death, there is this doubt that everyone has about him. Some say, 'He continues to exist,' while others say, 'He does not.' I want to know what happens in truth after death. Please let this be my third boon."

The god of Death was disturbed by this question, "Even the gods of old wanted to know the answer. Subtle and mysterious is the doctrine of life and death. Choose another boon and release me from answering this question."

Nachiketas grew more persistent, "You say that even the gods of old wanted to know. You say that the answer is most difficult. Yet who better a teacher can I find, O Death, than you? No other boon is equal to this."

Yama sought to dissuade Nachiketas by saying, "Do not make me answer this question, Nachiketas. I will give you instead children who will live a hundred years and multiply your lineage. I will give you countless livestock, horses and elephants, and plenty of gold."

Yama continued, "I will give you lordship over vast regions of this earth and let you live as many years as you wish. You may even choose to have great wealth, a long life, and great fame in this wide world, all at the same time. I will even grant you all your other desires. I will give you lovely maidens, accompanied by chariots and musical instruments, to attend to you. But do not ask me further about death, O Nachiketas."

Death was testing Nachiketas with the promise of a life of unlimited pleasures, but the boy was not to be deterred from his wish. "Keep your horses and maidens and songs and dances, O Death, and all other pleasures you have promised, for all these pleasures pass away. They only serve to sap the energy of life and our senses. Wealth does not make a man satisfied, and what use is wealth when you are in sight? What use is a long life when it means growing old in a place full of sorrow? Tell me what happens at the transition into the great beyond. I, Nachiketas, will not change my wish."

Now at last, Yama was willing to let Nachiketas know what happened to a person after death. It all depended on the choices that the person made throughout the life that preceded death. "Two paths lie before man," said Death, "the path of joy and the path of pleasure. The path of joy is the preferable path since it is the good path. The path of pleasure is an altogether different path. Good things await the person who chooses the preferable path because it is good for the person's well-being. The one who chooses the path of pleasure goes from death to death. The wise see the difference between these two paths and choose the path of joy over the path of pleasure. The fool chooses the pleasures that gratify over that which is beneficial."

And then Yama congratulated Nachiketas, "You, O Nachiketas, rejected the path laden with things that most people desire. You chose not to accept that chain of gold, lovely to behold, that binds human beings down so that they sink underneath. These two paths of wisdom and ignorance are widely different and lead to different ends. You, Nachiketas, are one who yearns for knowledge; the many pleasures do not tempt and confuse you. The ones who choose the path of gratifying their pleasures call themselves wise, even as they wallow in their ignorance."

Yama continued, "These fools stagger around in circles, wandering aimlessly, like the blind led by the blind. Deluded by their pursuit of wealth and pleasure, they fall into my clutches again and again. They go from death to death, ever deluded. The life that lies beyond death is beyond their reach . . . . When a person has heard and understood this truth, when he has grasped its subtlety, then he rises above pleasures and rejoices for he has found something to rejoice in. He goes beyond death and does not fall under my power again for he has chosen the path that leads to the source of unending joy."

The path of gratifying one's pleasures is simply unsustainable in the long term. As the lower bird seeks out sweet fruit that eventually sours, it is a fool's errand, forever unsatisfied, forever culminating in the death of one pleasure and the immediate birth of another. The Maitrī Upanishad reminds us that this journey of death to death takes place even in this one life that we know, as we live and die in anxiety and pain from one pleasure to the next. *Yet this is the model of insatiable growth in wants, year after year, that drives business and our economic system today.*

Compounding the Problem

There's a reason why it is so hard for us to understand Yama's lesson. Consider what Jeremy Grantham, the UK-born cofounder of the GMO Fund, has to say. He is one of the most famous and respected investors in the world, managing over $100 billion in investments through his asset management firm. His core message is that human beings cannot understand at a gut level the effects of compound growth.

Grantham gives a fascinating example of a discussion he had with mathematicians and other "superquants" who would presumably know the effects of year-after-year growth in material output:

> To point to the ludicrous unsustainability of this compound growth I suggested that we imagine the Ancient Egyptians . . . whose gods, pharaohs, language, and general culture lasted for well over 3,000 years. Starting with only a cubic meter of physical possessions, . . . I asked how much physical wealth they would have had 3,000 years later at 4.5% compounded growth. Now, these were trained mathematicians, so I teased them: "Come on, make a guess. Internalize the general idea. You know it's a very big number." . . . In fact, not one of these potential experts came within one billionth of 1% of the actual number, which is approximately 10^{57}, a number so vast that it could not be squeezed into a billion of our Solar Systems. . . . If trained mathematicians get it

so wrong, how can an ordinary specimen of Homo Sapiens have a clue? Well, he doesn't. . . . The bottom line really, though, is that no compound growth can be sustainable. Yet, how far this reality is from the way we live today, with our unrealistic levels of expectations and, above all, the optimistic outcomes that are simply assumed by our leaders.[11]

Time frames such as three thousand years are mind-boggling to consider. Yet it is worth remembering that the oldest Upanishads, still relevant today, were composed almost three thousand years ago. If world cultures still bear the influence of civilizations three millennia old, then *it is reasonable to expect that our underlying models of business are sustainable for at least a hundred years*—a mere fraction of our cultural models.

There's another reason why stewardship is so hard for us and why our impacts on nature are escalating. Nature provides a wide range of biodiversity and ecosystem services to business and humanity, such as fresh water, land, natural foods, fiber, disease and pest control, natural medicines, pollination, and climate regulation. However, the value of these services to companies is largely invisible to the decision makers because nature doesn't send us an invoice.

Instead, nature is thought of as a "public good" (or the commons) where public institutions such as the government are responsible for providing and managing it. But since these institutions have other interests, nature is typically left without a voice in the decision making. Similarly, the negative impacts of a company on the future ability of nature to provide these services are also invisible. As a result of these impacts, business creates *externalities* that are uncompensated, third-party costs imposed on nature because of economic activity.

Currently, the global economy receives $72 trillion worth of "free" goods and services from nature while creating $6.6 trillion in damages.[12] This damage is expected to grow to $28 trillion in 2050 with business as usual. Because of these free goods and externalities, nature faces a double whammy: its tenants don't pay their rent even as they trash the place. When we throw compound growth into the mix, you can see why many people are terrified at the direction this is going.

Here's another way to look at where we are going. We already consume services from nature at the rate of 1.5 Earths. At present rates of economic growth, we will need 2 Earths by 2030 and 5–7 Earths by 2050, which is when the millennial generation becomes middle-aged.[13] Our hard reality is that we have only one Earth to share—a cold fact that's not yet part of our business leadership models.

If the preferable path is the long-term path, then where can we turn for guidance on what this path may look like? The answer is simple in many cases: look to nature itself, which has had billions of years to devise its approach.

Learning from Nature

In the Upanishadic worldview, not only is a human being a steward of nature, but he or she can also gain wisdom about reality from it. A tale of a young seeker of wisdom named Satyakāma who learns about the highest reality from birds and animals and the natural elements is given in the Chāndogya Upanishad and summarized below. It is a story that emphasizes the wisdom of other nonhuman beings for seeking the Ātman.[14]

Satyakāma's teacher, Gautama, picked out four hundred emaciated and feeble cows and instructed the boy to take them away for feeding. (So much for instruction!) As Satyakāma led the cows away, he turned and said confidently, "When I return, I will have a thousand cows with me!" He lived away from the hermitage for many years and tended to the cows until they had increased in number to a thousand. The bull in the herd then called out to the boy, "Satyakāma, now that our herd has reached a thousand, we need to return. If you agree to lead us back, I will teach you a quarter portion of that which is ultimately real."[15] Satyakāma was overjoyed and said, "Sir, please teach me."

The bull then taught Satyakāma about the first quarter of reality: the four directions (east, west, south, and north). Over the course of his return journey, Satyakāma learned about the remaining three quarters of ultimate reality from other parts of nature: fire taught him about the quarter called Endless (earth, sky, ocean, and the space between), a goose taught him about the Luminous quarter (fire, the sun, the moon, and lightning), and a water bird showed him the part of reality that is Support-possessing (breath, sight, hearing, and the mind).

When Satyakāma finally returned to the hermitage, his teacher called out, "Satyakāma, you shine like a man who knows what is ultimately real. Tell me who taught it to you, my son!" Satyakāma told his teacher of what he had learned from the bull, the fire, the wild goose, and the water bird.[16]

The story of Satyakāma's instruction by nature's creatures is especially relevant in our world today, where nature is thought of as a resource to be exploited rather than a teacher we can learn from. If business leadership is to begin this difficult journey along the razor's edge of the preferable path that Death was talking about, the group to be moved first will need to be corporate investors. What seems to work is to focus on the business risks posed by increasingly unpredictable, limited, and expensive natural resources and other ecosystem services.

John Fullerton, founder of the Capital Institute, is a US-based investor who focuses on investing in the regeneration of natural systems. He left JP Morgan in 2001, just before the terrorist attacks of 9/11. He recalled:

I think experiencing 9/11 very much up close—I happened to be downtown that morning, the first time I'd been back downtown since I left working at Morgan—I think that sort of jolted me into . . . what I refer to as my "deep think period." . . . I really discovered the ecosystem crisis in a way I didn't expect and wasn't looking for. I had always really previously thought of environmental issues as these disconnected or unconnected "one-off" problems. You know, problems about a whale or an owl or something. But I was completely ignorant about the way the ecosystem works and any notion of finite limits and so reading *Limits to Growth* was very influential. . . . Reading E. F. Schumacher and Herman Daly and Hazel Henderson. There were all these people who were trying to work with the inconsistencies of how we know the biosystem works and the assumptions embedded in economic thinking.[17]

Describing a moment when he realized the limits of his ignorance, Fullerton said, "I was looking in the mirror one day and sort of looked there and said, 'It's all you,' meaning people like me who think they understand how the world works are really operating with some profoundly serious ignorance about how the world actually does work."[18]

Fullerton went on to explain how a debt-driven economic system demands precisely the kind of exponential growth the environment cannot withstand. He was heartened by the new approaches to economic thinking that address, according to him,

the physical impossibility of exponential growth as well as the unjust distribution of wealth that is being created by this system that tends to favor those with capital over those without capital. So it's sort of a two-pronged movement, but it's very much grounded in the physical-limit reality that was first talked about in *Limits to Growth*. Actually it was talked about before that, but that was sort of the work that put it in the mainstream in our current generation.[19]

He observed, "We're all complicit in a system that is ethically unsupportable." Yet this is a moment of great opportunity for leadership. "What are the chances that I happen to live at the time when we need to reinvent the whole economic system in order not to destroy ourselves?" He wondered, What if companies matured the way human beings do? At some point, physical growth would end while other forms of growth would continue. What if Wal-Mart grew into an oak tree?[20]

Despite the presence of investor-stewards such as Grantham and Fullerton, the investor community is still a long way away from insisting that business preserve and renew the natural elements of its larger context.[21] It seems that many more natural disasters will be needed to drive the need for Being-centered leadership home, unless many more Being-centered business leaders are inspired to lead by example as stewards.

TWEETS

- As stewards, we preserve and renew nature for the living beings after us for the simple reason that we are not nature's true owners.

- "I always make the case for sustainability. Our costs are down . . . our people are galvanized around a shared higher purpose."—Ray Anderson

- The key to stewardship is not to focus on it for its own sake, but to connect it to what the company has deeply cared about all its life.

- Being-centered business leaders recognize compounding effects and emphasize valuing the dependencies and impacts of business on nature.

- What if companies matured like humans and other living beings, where physical growth ends while other forms of growth continue?

SEEDS

- Why is it that we are willing to sacrifice a great deal personally for our children but don't see our stewardship of nature in the same way?

- What are some ways in which you could champion "zero-impact growth" and the valuation of the impacts of business on nature in your organization?

- What are some ways in which you could connect sustainability to a core strength of your company or something that its stakeholders care deeply about?

- What are some ways in which your company could grow, even as it matures into an oak tree that has slowed its material growth?

11

Leading as a Sage

By Being's sacred sound,
The wise reach that which is
Peaceful, beyond aging and death,
Fearless and ever supreme.
PRASHNA UPANISHAD

For the lower bird, the journey to the higher bird holds yet another possibility: the ability to fly directly to the trunk near where the higher bird rests. In the case of business, we have considered three different ways in which Being-centered leaders lead by example: as an inclusive materialist, as a humanist, and as a steward. But these ways can also be integrated within the same person, much like the tree trunk integrates all the tree's branches. Also, this integration often spans a long portion of one's life, much like the tree trunk spans the tree's life.

The key to such *integration* is a concept that shares the same meaning: *integrity*. The two are derived from the Greek words *integras* and *integritas,* which mean "making something whole and undivided again." In the same way that a tree trunk gives greater access to the whole tree, integrity enables leaders to acquire a larger knowledge of business as a whole, which is wisdom.

Integrity and wisdom together engender trust and the ability to inspire others through the power of personal example. A Being-centered leader then becomes a living sage because of his or her greater knowledge of the whole and ability to manifest it in all aspects of life. In essence, a business sage is one who shows *integrity and wisdom* across all the connections of business to its larger context, thereby coming closer to Being, or knowledge of the whole.

Three Sages

Consider Paul Polman, the Dutch-born CEO of Unilever, the giant consumer goods company, who once wanted to become a priest. He is a leader-sage who has set Unilever on a path to sustainable business that is exemplary. In doing so, he has taken risks that few CEOs are willing to take. The 2007–8 financial meltdown was a turning point in Polman's thinking, as was his realization of the global crises we are facing with regard to nature. To him, this is a "crisis of ethics" that compels leaders like him to reimagine capitalism and consider other ways of doing business.[1]

One of Polman's first acts as CEO of Unilever in 2009 was to get rid of quarterly reporting, which was the norm among European firms but was not required under the law. By doing so, he also got rid of the need to give quarterly earnings guidance to investors. While US public companies are required by law to report quarterly earnings, they are not required to provide quarterly earnings guidance to investors. As we saw earlier, this is nevertheless an entrenched business practice that drives short-term decisions by corporate leaders.

Polman was willing to take the daring step of stopping quarterly reporting because, as he said, "I figured I couldn't be fired on my first day."[2] This strategy of encouraging long-term investments has worked: ownership of Unilever shares by hedge funds—which tend to focus on short-term gains—dropped from 15 percent to 5 percent during 2009–13.[3]

As soon as he became CEO at Unilever, Polman gathered his colleagues and asked, "Why don't we develop a business model aimed at contributing to society and the environment instead of taking from them?"[4] He instituted other policies to ensure long-term thinking in Unilever, such as management incentives that encourage long-term performance, a broader focus on stakeholder well-being, and a strong long-term pipeline of innovations.

But these policy changes are not enough. As Polman has said, "They are necessary. But they are not sufficient. Changes in policy will mean little if not accompanied by changes in behavior. That's why we need a different approach to business—a new model led by a generation of leaders with the mind-set and the courage to tackle the challenges of the future."[5] In a world of growing needs where emerging countries are industrializing, what matters most is sustainable growth. According to Polman,

> The challenge for business is to meet these needs in a sustainable fashion. Success will require completely new business models. It will demand transformational innovation in product and process technologies to minimize resource use, as well as the development of "closed-loop" systems so that one man's waste becomes another's raw material.[6]

Unilever's vision for ensuring sustainable growth, the Sustainable Living Plan, seeks to double sales while halving Unilever's impacts on nature, improve the nutritional quality of its food products, and enable five hundred thousand small landholding farmers to make a sustainable living.

Polman's approach to business success is a good example of the long-term stakeholder well-being model of this book. He said:

> I don't think our fiduciary duty is to put shareholders first. I say the opposite. What we firmly believe is that if we focus our company on improving the lives of the world's citizens and come up with genuine sustainable solutions, we are more in synch with consumers and society and ultimately this will result in good shareholder returns.
>
> Why would you invest in a company which is out of synch with the needs of society, that does not take its social

compliance in its supply chain seriously, that does not think about the costs of externalities, or of its negative impacts on society?[7]

In the four years since Polman took over as CEO, Unilever's financial performance has been outstanding: its share price increased by 55 percent, its revenues grew by 25 percent, its operating costs reduced through streamlining its corporate structure, and it launched many new products and services.[8] By contrast, Unilever's main rival, Procter & Gamble fared considerably worse in terms of growth, overhead costs, product innovation, and corporate reputation.

Another business leader who is a sage is Jochen Zeitz, the former chairman and CEO of Puma, whose views on Being in business were shown in chapter 2. For Zeitz, Being-centered businesses emphasize an *ethical* foundation for stakeholder relationships to create a basis for mutual trust and high performance in the organization. While many companies preach such ethics, Zeitz and Puma have made a conscious effort to practice them in all their relationships with their stakeholders. The starting point for Puma is the belief that a business is Being centered when employees and other partners embed ethical thinking and integrity into their interactions with one another and with the natural world. Puma defines ethical interactions as being fundamentally fair, honest, positive, and creative—qualities it calls the 4Keys.

For Jochen Zeitz, ethical principles lead naturally to the importance of valuing the connections between business and its larger context. The challenge is to find a way that is tangible. As he said, "Because our connection to nature is hard to explain explicitly, we need to find ways to visualize and simplify it in our daily life. You have to come up with some tools to make it easier for us to deal with these connections. Not everybody's an Einstein. So, how do I connect the dots?"[9]

This search led him to pioneer the Environment Profit and Loss (E-P&L) approach, which puts a monetary value on the impacts and dependencies of business on nature. It's an approach that has the potential to transform business, especially by valuing the connections to nature that are otherwise invisible. As he said, "Obviously, we all enjoy the spirituality of nature and the cultural diversity of humans, but at the end of the day, how do you bring it into the day-to-day of business? By monetizing these values in a certain way, business can be much better at it rather than talk about the spiritual side of nature."[10] Zeitz is now working on a way to value the connections of business to humanity (the Social-P&L).

This emphasis on ethically guided practical principles has led to a string of visible successes for Puma. It was the first major corporation in the world to publicly disclose the economic costs of its impacts on the environment through the E P&L approach. It followed up this milestone by creating and leading a consortium of other global companies that plan to similarly disclose their economic impacts on nature. In a recent well-regarded ranking of the world's most sustainable companies, Puma was ranked as number two in the world after Unilever.[11] Not bad for a business executive who had once considered joining a monastery!

The experience of these companies suggests that the key to business success is a *corporate identity* led by ethical principles that puts sustainable growth at its center. In some work I did in 2011 of global corporations that were trying to be sustainable businesses, corporate identity emerged as the key means for implementing sustainable growth and for combining hardheaded and heartfelt business practices.[12] Other studies have also shown the value of corporate identity in enabling change.[13] This is because when corporate identity changes, how corporations view themselves and the world changes dramatically.[14] In turn, corporate identity is heavily influenced by the personal identity or sense of self of business leaders.

Let's consider one other leader-sage who is very well known in his home country of India and in the global IT industry but less known to the person on the street in the rest of the world: Azim Premji, the CEO of Wipro, the giant IT services company based in India.[15]

Premji took over the company upon his father's unexpected death in 1966. It was a transformative incident for him:

> My father died at the age of 51, when I was a student at Stanford University. As the male head of the family, I had to rush back home. At 21, I was appointed chief executive of the small company he'd formed. . . .
>
> . . . At the first shareholders' meeting, someone stood up and said: "Young man, my strong advice is that you sell your shares to a more mature holder. There's no way you can run a complex company like this."[16]

But Premji decided to hang on, determined to build on his father's legacy. From a maker of vegetable oils, Wipro moved into soaps, hair care, toiletries, and hydraulic cylinders before finding its groove in the IT hardware and software services industry in the 1990s. Wipro grew rapidly in the next twenty years and is now the second-largest IT services company in India—employing over one hundred and forty thousand employees across almost sixty countries.

Wipro is a terrific financial success by any standards, generating revenues of over $7 billion and profits of over $1 billion in 2012 while providing a wide range of business outsourcing services to companies.

Premji's story is remarkable because of his efforts over nearly half a century to pursue values-based excellence at Wipro, as well as his appreciation of the larger context of business. For example, *BusinessWeek* chose him as one of the top thirty all-time great entrepreneurs globally, while Wipro has won numerous honors as one of the most ethical and sustainable companies in the world.[17]

One of Premji's distinctive traits is his humility. It is something he believes in deeply. In his mind, "Excellence requires humility. This is especially needed when we feel we have reached the peak of excellence and there is nothing further we can do."[18] He follows up these beliefs with his actions. He is known widely for his simple and unassuming lifestyle, preferring to stay in ordinary hotels rather than the five-star extravaganzas that have spread throughout India.

He chooses to purchase locally made clothes and watches and uses modest cars that give no inkling at all that he is India's third-richest person, with his personal wealth estimated at over $13 billion in 2013. In 2012, in a show of luxury for him, he traded in his modest Toyota car for a secondhand Mercedes-Benz. He is known for his quiet and unassuming presence at work, choosing to stay behind the scenes and preferring to listen at staff meetings rather than dominate them.

His way of being transforms people around him and puts into practice what he has said about leadership:

> One of the most important qualities that build an organization is leadership. The most important ingredient that goes into making a leader successful is powerful personal credibility. Leaders must deliver on their commitment and must be able to generate collective enthusiasm.[19]

Premji is also a man of great integrity, insisting that his company neither accept nor give bribes (even though corruption is rampant in India), and expects that his employees demonstrate integrity at work. In one incident, he fired an employee for claiming expenses for first-class train travel while actually traveling second class. He refused to back down even when the employee's union went on a strike for three months.

To be honest, when I read such favorable descriptions by and about business leaders, I tend to be skeptical. But what is remarkable about Azim Premji is that these qualities are actual in his case, as I know directly from old friends who have worked closely with him over many years.

What I also find most impressive about Premji is the great generosity with which he has shared his wealth with Indian society. In 2001, he established a foundation to promote universal education in India, especially in the rural areas, with the mission to create a more just, humane, and equitable society. He followed up by contributing $4.4 billion to it, making him the most generous man in Asia and among the top five in the world, according to *Forbes*.[20]

Of the $4.4 billion, about $2 billion was pledged in early 2013, weeks after he announced that he was signing the Giving Pledge, the initiative by Warren Buffett and Bill Gates to persuade the world's richest to give away much of their wealth. Premji had hosted Buffett and Gates in India and was acting on his pledge.

The Azim Premji Foundation has partnered with tens of thousands of schools, hundreds of colleges, and millions of schoolchildren. The new gift would enable it to scale up considerably through programs at the district and state levels, as well as expand Azim Premji University. The plan was to build fifty to one hundred demonstration schools at the district level, while the foundation's headcount was expected to grow from eight hundred to four to five thousand people. It shows all signs of becoming one of the most important foundations for public education in the world, a remarkable testament to the generosity of a humble, persistent, values-driven man who strove for excellence and built one of the great technology services companies in the world.

Two Ways of Prospering

Being-centered leader-sages such as Paul Polman, Jochen Zeitz, and Azim Premji (respectively a Christian who almost became a priest, an existential philosopher who spent time in a monastery, and a Muslim who almost joined the World Bank[21]) represent a well-balanced synthesis of leadership qualities because of their focus on the higher relationships and shared purpose of business.

For a sage, the lower bird in the tree of business life connects directly and steadily to the higher bird because the higher bird embodies integrity and radiates trust. These qualities have become absolutely critical because of the erosion of societal trust in business since the financial crisis of 2008. Business leadership urgently needs to address the widespread public perception that companies prosper at the cost of society.

A delightful tale in the Chāndogya Upanishad that tells about two different ways of prospering is relevant here.[22] In a town in ancient India lived a man named Jānaśruti. He was a rich man who built many homes for the aged and infirm and fed many people. But these many charities were like investments to him, since he often thought, "I will gather the merit that comes from giving to others and from the good things that they themselves do."

In the culture of ancient India, gathering the merit of others referred to the buildup of one's own good fortune in the future (*karma*) through the good deeds performed for others. One night as Jānaśruti stood outside his home, some geese flew overhead on their way to distant lands. Jānaśruti could understand the language of the geese since it was a merit he had gathered through his investments.

One of the geese said to another, "Hey there, Bright-Eyes! Look at that light that spreads throughout the sky like the light from Jānaśruti! Beware lest you get burned by its brightness." But the other scoffed at this comparison and said, "Not so fast! How can you speak of Jānaśruti's glow as though he were Raikva, the great gatherer of merit?"

Surprised, the first bird asked, "Why do you speak thus of Raikva?" Bright-Eyes replied, "Just as the winner of the dice game gathers all the bids from the lower throws, so does Raikva gather merit from all the good that people do. And those who know what Raikva knows, likewise gather merit."

Jānaśruti was much troubled by what he had overheard. The next morning, he called his chief assistant to his side and relayed what the geese had said. He then asked him to search the town to find this person called Raikva, who was very likely from the learned classes. The assistant searched every place where the learned classes lived but could not find him. Jānaśruti then instructed him, "Perhaps he is not a learned man after all. Search for him where the other social classes live."

After searching high and low in neighboring villages, the assistant was at last directed to a man under a cart who was contentedly scratching himself. He asked respectfully, "Are you Raikva, the gatherer of merit?" The man replied calmly, "Yes, I am Raikva." The assistant returned home to say that Raikva had at last been found.

Jānaśruti, generous in both charity and greed, went to Raikva with six hundred cows, a fine carriage, and a gold necklace and said, "Raikva, take these cows, carriage and necklace made of gold. In return, sir, please teach me what you know." But Raikva retorted, "Hey, you! Take your cows and carriage, and a fine necklace made of gold and return to your home. I do not want them."

Jānaśruti went away and pondered what to do next. He then returned to Raikva and said, "Raikva, here are a thousand cows, a fine carriage, a gold necklace, and my daughter's hand in marriage, and here is the title to the village where you live. Please, sir, teach me what you know." Raikva turned down these inducements but agreed this time to reveal his wisdom to Jānaśruti:

> In the natural world, the great gatherer clearly is the wind. When a fire goes out, its smoke and ashes pass into the wind. When the sun and the moon set, they pass into the wind. When water evaporates, it passes into the wind. Everything in the natural world eventually passes into the wind.
>
> In the same way, the great gatherer for this human body is the life breath. When a man sleeps, his speech passes into his breath. His sight, mind and hearing similarly pass into his breath. Everything in this body eventually passes into the life breath.
>
> These are the two great gatherers in the world—the life breath among the vital functions of the body, and the wind among the universal elements. Whoever knows this connection between the wind in the world and the life breath in the human body knows how to benefit when others benefit.[23]

Here again we see the principle of correspondence of the Upanishads. The person who knew and felt (as Raikva felt deeply through his life outdoors) the hidden relationships between human beings and nature had treasure beyond measure. Moreover, what a strange and wonderful way to draw out the distinction between Jānaśruti's way of gathering merit and Raikva's!

Jānaśruti's way may be described as social investments with the intention of building his reputation as a generous person. While these investments were laudable, their ultimate intent was to gather fame that was greater than that of others in society. It is similar to the way in which many corporations approach sustainability—that is, as corporate social responsibility that helps build a corporate reputation that is better than others'.

This is why Jānaśruti was very troubled when one of the geese extolled the virtues of Raikva. His main concern was to ensure that he could restore his original reputation by learning Raikva's secret to gathering merit. For Jānaśruti, reputation was a zero-sum game that never seemed to end.

Raikva, on the other hand, had an entirely different way of acquiring merit. It came from an understanding of the deep connection among himself, his fellow beings, the natural elements, and the underlying force that ultimately shaped this world. He did not care a whit about his reputation or his relative position compared to others.

For Raikva, reputation was not a zero-sum game. He did what he did for its own sake and not because of how it looked to others. Moreover, the kind of wealth he accumulated was freedom, not material gain—the great freedom to rest happily under a cart while untouched by the anxieties of the world. His refusal to reveal his secrets in exchange for material wealth showed a very different mind-set.

Another difficulty in Jānaśruti's way of dispensing prosperity is that it does not address the way in which the original wealth was created in the first place. Often, the subsequent charities (while laudable) can become a way to justify wealth created in ways that violate the dharma of business leadership I described earlier.

The wealth creation that illustrates a Being-centered approach is one where the long-term stakeholder well-being is improved from the *beginning* of the wealth-creation process. By involving key stakeholders from the beginning and considering their different levels of identity or sense of self, the wealth cocreated by business is real, relevant, and long lasting. I am an affiliated scholar at Stanford University's Kozmetsky Global Collaboratory, where we are defining such wealth as *shareable prosperity* and exploring how it can be created where it is most needed. Shareable prosperity begins with a mind-set that is Being centered, where a sense of inner abundance leads to shared external prosperity.

When wealth is created in ways that do not add real value to society, economists call it *rent seeking*. It is defined as "getting income not as a reward [for] creating wealth but by grabbing a larger share of the wealth that would otherwise have been produced without their effort."[24] Rather than create new wealth, rent seekers take wealth away from others. Under rent seeking, wealth acquisition becomes a zero-sum game where there are winners and losers. As a result, private gain is not aligned with societal gain.[25]

There are grounds for arguing that many important business innovations in the financial sector in the last thirty years have relied on rent seeking rather than real improvements in business productivity or efficiency.[26] These innovations have been directed at increasing monopoly power, circumventing government regulations, taking advantage of imperfections in the marketplace, and enabling unequal access to relevant information.

As a result, the gap between the richest 1 percent and the remaining 99 percent of US society has widened, as it has elsewhere in many other countries in the world. However, some sages among us use their position and influence to actively work to shrink that gap. One is the Sage of Omaha.

The Sage of Omaha

One of the most famous sages in business is Warren Buffett, the legendary US investor and second-richest person in America. He is called the Sage of Omaha for the great foresight he has shown over the many decades he has been in business in picking the right stocks. How does he stack up against the requirements of a living sage, according to Being-centered leadership?

Buffett's investment results show clearly that he is the example par excellence of long-term investing. During 1965–2012, the per-share book value of Berkshire Hathaway has grown by over 587,000 percent, compared to the S&P 500 growth of almost 7,400 percent. This means that if you had invested a mere $200 in Buffett's company in 1965, you would have become a millionaire in 2012, compared to having gained around $15,000 if you had invested in the S&P 500.[27]

Buffett has perfected the technique of value investing, where investors look for stocks whose external valuation is low compared to their intrinsic value. Berkshire-Hathaway is one of the very few US public companies that has followed and stayed with a long-term shareholder value model.[28]

Buffett's unique skill is in consistently locating companies with high intrinsic value that go unrecognized by other investors. See's Candy is a remarkable example of Buffett's ability to identify long-term opportunities and stay with them. An initial investment of $25 million in 1972 to purchase the company outright, followed by additional investments of $32 million, resulted in over $1.3 billion in pretax earnings by 2007.

Aside from creating wealth for everyone he's been associated with, Buffett is also an incomparable humanist and a man of great integrity. His decision to give away all his wealth to charity after his death, his active efforts to get billionaires to give away half of their wealth to social and other causes, and his public support for bringing more equity into the tax code (the "Buffett Rule") are all examples of a profoundly wise and generous humanist. It is a tragedy that while many claim to worship him, far fewer follow his investment approach.

Buffett is a wonderful role model for a sage who thinks long term, cares about all his stakeholders, and feels a strong connection to humanity. But one important thing is missing. For a man of Buffett's prodigious wisdom, talents, and foresight, its absence is remarkable. The environment is hardly ever explicitly discussed, and while much long-term strategy is undeniably behind Buffett's work, the impact of business decisions on our already-fragile ecosystems represents a hole in his great vision. It is something I just cannot explain.

Looking through Buffett's famous reports to shareholders, it is hard to see a real discussion of the risks of climate change or ecosystem loss, even though these risks are very real for many of Berkshire Hathaway's businesses. One of the industries hardest hit by climate change disruptions will be insurance services, and Berkshire owns some of the best and largest of these companies.

But Buffett has very little to say about nature in his hugely anticipated annual reports to shareholders. For example, here's what he had to say in his March 1, 2013, report about possible insurance losses for the reinsurance group that is one of the stars of his portfolio: "If the insurance industry should experience a $250 billion loss from some mega-catastrophe—a loss about triple anything it has ever experienced—Berkshire as a whole would likely record a significant profit for the year because it has so many streams of earnings."[29]

This is similar to what he has said in previous years. It's striking because it does not discuss any of the likely causes of these insurance losses, such as climate change, ecosystem destruction, or loss in asset values due to future concerns or regulations about the impacts of business on nature. Many of these impacts will occur within the next decade, a timeline well within Buffett's long-range horizon.

For this wise and generous sage who says, "I try to look out ten or twenty years when making an acquisition, but sometimes my eyesight has been poor,"[30] this lack of explicit recognition of the risks from the loss of nature is a brilliantly visible blind spot. I find it hard to understand. If Buffett were a far more active steward of nature than he is now, he may well have been the foremost leader-sage among all modern business leaders—the Pericles of this Neoaxial Age of business.

Perfection is hard to expect, even in a modern oracle. But I know that when Omaha's sage puts on his battle gear to also do nature's battle or sound its trumpets, as Polman, Zeitz, Premji, and other business leaders have done, a great number of business leaders will follow.

TWEETS

- A business sage shows integrity and wisdom across all connections of business to its larger context, thereby coming closer to Being.

- "We need . . . a new model led by a generation of leaders with the mind-set and the courage to tackle the challenges of the future."—Paul Polman

- Being-centered leaders emphasize an *ethical* foundation for stakeholder relationships to create mutual trust and high performance.

- The key to business success is a *corporate identity* that puts sustainable growth at its center.

- "The most important ingredient that goes into making a leader successful is powerful personal credibility." —Azim Premji

- Shareable prosperity improves stakeholder well-being from the beginning of wealth creation instead of distributing at the end as charity.

SEEDS

- What are the lessons you can learn from Paul Polman's courage and initiatives to implement a new model of sustainable business growth?

- What are the lessons you can learn from Jochen Zeitz's emphasis on ethical principles as a basis for all interactions with stakeholders?

- What are the lessons you can learn from Azim Premji's emphasis on humility and personal credibility as a business leader?

- What do you think it would take for Warren Buffett to lead on nature?

Freedom

By the Self that is like an inner light,
The one who realizes Being
Is freed from all constraints
Because of that which is
Eternal, unchanging, and pure.

ŚVETĀŚVATARA UPANISHAD

Real Business Freedom

Beyond the unmanifest is Being:
All-pervading Person, free of attributes,
The one who knows this Person
Attains freedom and life eternal.

KAṬHA UPANISHAD

In the previous chapters, I talked of Being-centered leadership mainly in the context of the journey of the lower bird toward the higher bird that is Being. The four stages of Being-centered leadership describe the lower bird's journey to be near to and realize the higher bird in the tree of business life. This is a journey that could take a lifetime to pursue because of the great challenge of transcending the hold of the lower, material self in us, but the rewards along the journey make it worthwhile. Not the least of these rewards is a business that recognizes a higher purpose; is less obsessed with short-term, material profits; and begins to nurture its connections to humanity and nature.

By our seeking to realize the higher bird of business leadership, the storms raging around us—of climate change and loss of ecosystems and biodiversity, of a loss of public trust in the integrity of business, of workplace alienation, of growing inequalities in society, and many others—begin to quiet down gradually.

A business that is reconnecting to the world improves the well-being of every stakeholder. But Being-centered leadership applies not just to businesses and business leaders but also to other areas of our lives. It applies to individuals as well as groups and to how we respond to crises, natural and manmade. Moreover, each stage need not go well nor transcend the particular challenge, as the lower bird in us struggles to make the journey to the higher bird through the slips and falls of uncertain branches. Though the climb is difficult and continuous, the will to advance grows with each new glimpse of sky.

Although biology ensures that leaders cannot be fully disembodied from their material self, *the higher bird of Being becomes the guiding light for engaging with the world.* When business leaders recognize, experience, anchor in, and lead by example with this higher bird as the guiding light, they achieve freedom from the constraints of the lower bird, as well as the freedom to pursue the greater opportunities of the higher bird. This freedom *from* and freedom *to* is the true promise of Being-centered leadership.

Speaking of biology, the analyst in me can't help but speculate why our sense of Being first arose and continues to have such a hold on us. Perhaps it is a cultural response to our lack of experience in adapting to the rapidly increasing power we are acquiring over our world. After all, fish don't despoil their water, birds seldom foul their nests, and wild animals rarely destroy their own forest.

Industrializing man is like an army of ants equipped with bulldozers as it races through the forest floor. Being is perhaps our own way to put constraints on our powers, where evolution did not give us enough time to adapt wisely to this much-too-rapid empowerment. Anyhow, while constraints seem restrictive as a concept, those that limit the damage we can do may actually give us more freedom.

Real business freedom (and *real capitalism*) is based on a holistic view of the connections of business to humanity, nature, and Being. Where the value of these connections is not factored into the decision-making and measurement systems of business, the higher reality of business is ignored. When the success of business leadership is defined narrowly in terms of satisfying the material interests of shareholders, other key aspects of well-being and other stakeholders are neglected. As a result, a less-than-holistic view means that business reality has been distorted, which in turn constrains business freedom.

These many distortions of business reality, described in previous chapters, include not recognizing the unintended consequences (or externalities) of business, overemphasizing material capital over other forms of capital, and relying on short-term over long-term considerations. They also include overemphasizing the material interests of a few stakeholders such as shareholders, while not recognizing the needs of other stakeholders. Other distortions include not recognizing the value of higher purpose and meaning for employees and not adding real value to society but engaging in "rent seeking."

Still others include overemphasizing competitive comparison because of an insecure self and anchoring in measures of success that are based on short-term pleasure rather than sustained delight. And they include not recognizing the damage caused to nature because of business, as well as the damage caused to society by excessive economic inequality. This is a long list that *urgently* demands we improve capitalism and business, despite the great value they have provided us.

The great irony of leadership is that with these distortions of business reality, the existing business leadership models of free-enterprise capitalism are anything but free. The stories from the Upanishads emphasize that true freedom is very different. It is freedom from self-engendered constraints such as excessive material desires, sorrow, unintended consequences, ignorance, vested interests, and the fear of change. It is also the freedom *to* pursue opportunities such as the perfecting of business, and to know and become who you truly are.[1]

Most of all, it is the opportunity to release the full potential of business for driving positive change in the world. It is the freedom to leave an inspiring legacy by helping make business the most important force for creating the greatest good in the world. Such real freedom comes from an undistorted view of business reality—a holistic vision that fully recognizes business's connections to the world. This, rather than the distorted version we see today, is what real capitalism is about.

At the same time, business leaders who take a holistic view of business and its connections run into great difficulties because the underlying model of business is complicit in this distortion of business reality. If there has to be real change, nothing less than the *full engagement* of business leaders is needed. As a result, the choice for business leaders is relatively clear: engage fully as leaders or engage as usual as managers.

The key difference between management and leadership is that managers seek to be optimal within the constraints of the existing business model, while leaders have the *courage* to question the existing model of business itself. What the world needs now, even more than managers who optimally manage what can be measured externally, are leaders who courageously lead because they are inspired internally.

The stages of the REAL road map are the mind's rationalization of the faint glimpse of Being that nature provides us through threads more ancient than humanity itself. If we could only listen closely, nature overflows with the birdsongs of Being. Humans added more threads to this web of connection first spun by Being and nature, threads now at risk of being cut with unprecedented haste as business disconnects itself from the world. To practice Being-centered leadership is to participate once again in the ancient and glorious tradition of repairing and weaving new threads in this world of interconnected beings. It is the equivalent of the great Hebrew concept of *tikkun olam* (repairing the world).

Āruṇi and Śvetaketu, Yājñavalkya and Maitreyī, King Janaka, Bhrigu and Varuṇa, Indra and Prajāpati, Raikva and Jānaśruti, Nachiketas and Yama, and Satyakāma—these are the people of the Upanishads, with names unpronounceable even for many Indian tongues, who participated in this weaving almost three thousand years ago. They were joined by a mélange of animals and natural elements to connect us to Being. In our more modern story, the twenty-one leaders of corporations discussed in this book have shown small and large touches of Being-centered leadership, whether they believed in Being or not.

These modern business leaders and their companies are listed here in the order they were introduced: Anita Roddick (the Body Shop), Jeffrey Swartz (Timberland), Jochen Zeitz (Puma), Indra Nooyi (PepsiCo), Herb Kelleher (Southwest Airlines), Alessandro Carlucci (Natura Cosméticos), Dr. V (Aravind Eye Care System), Colman Mockler (Gillette), Jim Sinegal (Costco), Father Arizmendi (Mondragon), Ursula Burns (Xerox), Chip Conley (Joie de Vivre Hotels), James Burke (Johnson & Johnson), Lars Sørensen (Novo Nordisk), Ray Anderson (Interface), Eileen Fisher (Eileen Fisher), Jeremy Grantham (GMO Fund), John Fullerton (Capital Institute), Paul Polman (Unilever), Azim Premji (Wipro), and Warren Buffett (Berkshire Hathaway).

But this is only a partial list, peopled by my own personal preferences. Another thing to remember: although the people listed are almost all CEOs, *Being-centered leaders come at all levels of the organizational hierarchy.*

I've used ancient and modern stories to describe the great quest of the lower bird within every one of us to realize the higher bird that is our inner presence. This higher bird is the shining, golden-hued truth of the Upanishads—the end goal of our aspirations, the universal self that is Being itself. Ultimately, it is immaterial whether we call it Ātman, Being, or something else because names are meager means through which we label a deeper truth.

When leaders seek this Being through humanity and nature—or directly—they embark on a courageous journey to make business and capitalism truly real. It is an ancient quest that transformed Axial Age societies and can now transform business by reconnecting it to the world. *There is no leadership journey of greater existential importance than this*, to realize the higher bird in the tree of business life and make business whole and free.

The one who pursues this quest, even if imperfectly, can truly be called a Being-centered leader, a seeker of Being itself.

TWEETS

- When business leaders recognize, experience, anchor in, and lead by example with Being as their guide, they set business truly free.

- Real business freedom (and real capitalism) is based on a holistic view of the connections of business to humanity, nature, and Being.

- Being-centered leaders leave an inspiring legacy to make business the most important force for creating the greatest good in the world.

- Being-centered leaders participate in the ancient tradition of repairing and weaving new threads in a world of interconnected beings.

- There is no leadership journey of greater existential importance than to make business whole and free through Being-centered leadership.

SEEDS

- What does *true freedom* mean in the context of rights and responsibilities with regard to capitalism and modern corporations?

- What do you think are the most important barriers to the adoption of the REAL road map by business leaders? By you in your organization?

- What is our responsibility as a civilization to ancient civilizations that saw the world as one of interconnected beings?

- What do *you* think is the business leadership journey of existential importance?

NOTES

Foreword

1. South Asia Institute, "Mapping India's Kumbh Mela," Harvard University, accessed May 7, 2013, http://southasiainstitute.harvard .edu/kumbh-mela/mapping-indias-kumbh-mela/.

Introduction

1. Potsdam Institute for Climate Impact Research and Climate Analytics, *Turn Down the Heat: Why a 4°C World Must Be Avoided* (Washington, DC: World Bank, November 2012). According to the Intergovernmental Panel on Climate Change's 2007 and 2012 assessments, almost 60 percent of the greenhouse gas emissions leading to climate change are due to industrial activity related to energy supply, manufacturing, and transportation. The rest are from forestry, agriculture, commercial and residential buildings, and wastewater treatment/use.

2. Estimates of species extinction due to human activity vary widely. See "Mass Extinction Underway," last updated March 7, 2013, http://www.mysterium.com/extinction.html, for an extensive listing. One commonly reported estimate is by the eminent biologist E. O. Wilson, who expects 50 percent of all species to be extinct by 2100. While 1.5 million species have already been discovered, the actual numbers could range from 10 to 100 million, which means 5 to 50 million species could become extinct by 2100.

3. United Nations Children's Fund, *The State of the World's Children: Special Edition* (New York: UNICEF, 2009), http://www.unicef.org /rightsite/sowc/pdfs/SOWC_Spec%20Ed_CRC_Main%20Report _EN_090409.pdf.

4. DARA and the Climate Vulnerable Forum, *Climate Vulnerability Monitor: A Guide to the Cold Calculus of a Hot Planet* (Madrid:

DARA, 2012), http://daraint.org/wp-content/uploads/2012/09 /CVM2-Low.pdf.

5. Nikki Blacksmith and Jim Harter, "Majority of American Workers Not Engaged in Their Jobs," Gallup Wellbeing, October 28, 2011, http://www.gallup.com/poll/150383/majority-american-workers-not -engaged-jobs.aspx.

6. Joseph Stiglitz, *The Price of Inequality: How Today's Divided Society Endangers Our Future* (New York: W. W. Norton, 2012), 3.

7. "2013 Edelman Trust Barometer: Executive Summary," Scribd, http://www.scribd.com/doc/121501475/Executive-Summary -2013-Edelman-Trust-Barometer.

8. "Environmental Concerns 'At Record Lows': Global Poll," GlobeScan Radar, February 25, 2013, http://www.globescan.com/commentary -and-analysis/press-releases/press-releases-2013/261-environmental -concerns-at-record-lows-global-poll.html.

9. See Jonathan Haidt, *The Happiness Hypothesis: Finding Modern Truth in Ancient Wisdom* (New York: Basic Books, 2006), for a great description of why we are mostly driven by emotions and rarely by reason. Especially interesting is the metaphor of an elephant (automatic processing) and the elephant rider (conscious verbal thinking) to describe our behavior.

10. See Thomas McEvilley, *The Shape of Ancient Thought: Comparative Studies in Greek and Indian Philosophies* (New York: Allworth Press, 2002), 33 for a discussion.

11. The spread of Being-related ideas in the West can be seen in the attention given to them in the twentieth century by philosophers such as Martin Heidegger (*Being and Time*), Jean-Paul Sartre (*Being and Nothingness*), and Ken Wilber (*Integral Spirituality*); psychologists such as Abraham Maslow (*Toward a Psychology of Being*) and Erich Fromm (*On Having and Being*); and popular writers such as E. F. Schumacher (*A Guide for the Perplexed*) and Eckhart Tolle (*The Power of Now*).

12. The Muktikopanishad alone lists 108 Upanishads, while several other texts such as the Bhagavad Gītā may also be considered as Upanishads. The Upanishads are part of the Vedas, the sacred literature of the Vedic religion of ancient India. The Vedas themselves

comprised two portions: (1) The *karma-kāṇḍa*, or the ritual portion, comprising the *saṃhitās* (hymns) and the Brāhmaṇas (liturgies), and (2) The *jñāna-kāṇḍa*, or the knowledge portion, comprising the Upanishads. Four important Vedic texts—Rig, Yajur, Sama and the Atharva—formed the *saṃhitās*. The Rig Veda, composed during 1500–1200 BCE, is the oldest Indo-European literature that is still in use today. Another set of Vedic texts, the Āraṇyakas, is often grouped with the Upanishads because of their similarity.

13. See McEvilley, *The Shape of Ancient Thought*, for a fascinating and thorough analysis of how the early Upanishads influenced the pre-Socratic philosophers of ancient Greece such as Thales (the father of Western philosophy), Anaximenes, Anaximander, Pythagoras, Xenophanes, Parmenides, and others during the period 600–450 BCE.

14. Fascinatingly, some speculate that the word *entrepreneur* may ultimately be derived from the Sanskrit phrase *antah prerna* (inner inspiration). See Gregory Hosono, "Entrepreneurship in 500 Words," *Huffington Post*, November 5, 2011, http://www.huffingtonpost.com /gregory-hosono/entrepreneurship-in-500-w_b_1077954.html.

Chapter 1

1. The metaphor of the two birds as representing the two selves in the human body is specifically used in the Muṇḍaka (3.1.1–2) and Śvetāśvatara (4.6–7) Upanishads. They derived this metaphor from an even more ancient image of two birds that first appeared in the Rig Veda *saṃhitā* 1.164.20–22 (1500–1200 BCE).

2. While the verse does not literally specify the relative heights of the two birds in the tree, interpreters have assumed them to be at two different levels that depend on their spiritual maturity.

3. Technically, the Sanskrit word for *Being* in ancient Indian philosophy was *Sat*. However, the Upanishads emphasize that *Brahman*, the foundational reality of this world, is also *Being* or *Sat*. Similarly, *Sat* is also considered as reality in the Upanishads. To prevent further confusion, I define *Being* as *Brahman* and *reality* as *Sat* in this book.

4. See Louis Fry and Mark Kriger, "Toward a Theory of Being-Centered Leadership: Multiple Levels of Being as Context for Effective

Leadership," *Human Relations* 62, no. 11 (2009) for an excellent academic introduction to the subject in the context of business leadership. Fry and Kriger identify five levels of being-centered leadership. The Being-centered (with a capital *B*) leadership described in this book corresponds to the highest and most difficult level of Fry and Kriger's hierarchy.

5. See Karl Jaspers, *The Origin and Goal of History* (New York: Routledge, 2011). While this book focuses on the wisdom of the Upanishads, it is important to recognize that these texts were representative of the wisdom of the Axial Age. As Karen Armstrong pointed out in *The Great Transformation: The Beginning of Our Religious Traditions* (New York: Alfred A. Knopf, 2006), viii, "The people of India were always in the vanguard of Axial progress."

6. See Armstrong, *The Great Transformation*, for details of the unprecedented violence, turmoil, natural calamity, and conquests of 1600–530 BCE that preceded and spilled over into the Axial Age. Historian A. L. Basham described this period in India (in *The Wonder That Was India* [New York: Grove Press, 1954], 246), in terms that make it appear strikingly similar to our current global situation:

> The time of which we speak was one of great social change, when old tribal units were breaking up. . . . Despite the great growth of material civilization at the time, the hearts of many men were failing them for fear of what should come to pass upon earth. It is chiefly to this deep feeling of insecurity that we must attribute the growth of pessimism.

7. See Patrick Olivelle, trans., *Upaniṣads* (New York: Oxford University Press, 1996), especially the introduction, for an excellent discussion of the real meaning of the Upanishads in terms of hidden connections. In general, I have chosen to rely on this meaning because of Olivelle's recognition in the West as a preeminent Sanskrit scholar and authority on the Upanishads. I've also relied on this translation by Olivelle for narrating the stories from the Upanishads that are included in this book.

8. The empathy described in the Upanishads is strikingly consistent with what modern science tells us about how mirror neurons work in our brain.

9. For example, see George Lakoff and Mark Johnson, *Philosophy in the Flesh: The Embodied Mind and Its Challenge to Western Thought* (New York: Basic Books, 1999), for a description of the central role of metaphors in determining how the mind works.

10. In the Upanishads, one central theme is that Brahman is Ātman; that is, the transcendent reality is none other than the immanent universal self.

11. Jumana Farouky, "Anita Roddick, the Queen of Green," *Time*, September 11, 2007, http://www.time.com/time/business/article /0,8599,1660911,00.html.

12. Scott Allen, "Anita Roddick—Redefining Business as We Know It," About.com Entrepreneurs, http://entrepreneurs.about.com/od /famousentrepreneurs/p/anitaroddick.htm.

13. "About Dame Anita Roddick," AnitaRoddick.com, accessed April 22, 2013, http://www.anitaroddick.com/aboutanita.php.

14. "Biography of Anita Roddick," Great Entrepreneurs, MyPrimeTime, accessed May 20, 2013, http://www.myprimetime.com/work/ge /roddickbio/.

15. "About Dame Anita Roddick."

16. Ibid. and Farouky, "Anita Roddick."

17. "About Dame Anita Roddick."

18. Farouky, "Anita Roddick."

19. Robert Eccles, Ioannis Ioannou, and George Serafeim, "The Impact of a Corporate Culture of Sustainability on Corporate Behavior and Performance" (working paper 12-035, *Harvard Business School*, November 25, 2011), http://www.hbs.edu/faculty/Publication%20 Files/12-035.pdf.

20. Ibid.

21. Ram Nidumolu, C. K. Prahalad, and M. R. Rangaswami, "Why Sustainability Is Now the Key Driver of Innovation," *Harvard Business Review*, September 2009.

22. According to the HBS study by Eccles, Ioannou, and Serafeim, this outperformance is strongest in consumer markets, where firms compete based on brands and reputation or where products use a lot of natural resources.

Chapter 2

1. This self is now the subject of much research on consciousness in neuroscience and psychology. For example, see Antonio Damasio, *Self Comes to Mind* (New York: Pantheon Books, 2010).

2. Sarvepalli Radhakrishnan, *The Principal Upanishads* (New York: Humanity Books, 1992), 73.

3. For a fascinating treatment of how this sense of separation from the world was accelerated since the Enlightenment and the Industrial Revolution by an increasingly dominant left brain in humans, see Iain McGilchrist, *The Master and His Emissary* (New Haven: Yale University Press, 2010). The left brain and the right brain are like the two birds, distinguished by separation versus engagement, part versus the whole, the abstracted versus the contextual, and so on.

4. See Raj Sisodia, David Wolfe, and Jagdish Sheth, *Firms of Endearment* (Upper Saddle River, NJ: Wharton School Publishing, 2007), 255.

5. VF Corporation, "VF Completes Acquisition of The Timberland Company," press release, September 18, 2011, http://www.vfc .com/news/press-releases?nws_id=ACD3A724-6461-2098-E043 -A740E3EA2098.

6. In the Upanishads, the principle of correspondence is frequently invoked to connect nature to animals and human beings. For example, the opening verses of the Brihad-āranyaka Upanishad describe the connection between a horse and nature (as translated in Olivelle, *Upaniṣads*, 7):

> The head of the sacrificial horse, clearly, is the dawn—its sight is the sun; its breath is the wind; and its gaping mouth is the fire common to all men. The body of the sacrificial horse is the year—its back is the sky; its abdomen is the intermediate region; its underbelly is the earth; its flanks are the quarters . . . its feet are the days and nights; its bones are the stars; its flesh is the clouds; its stomach contents are the sand; its intestines are the rivers. . . . When it yawns, lightning flashes; when it shakes itself, it thunders; and when it urinates, it rains. Its neighing is speech itself.

The ancient sage Yājñavālkya, whose exploits and wisdom are central to the Brihad-āraṇyaka Upanishad, gives a detailed analogy to illustrate the hidden correspondence between a human being and a tree (as translated in Valerie Roebuck, *The Upanishads* [London: Penguin Books, 2003], 59):

> Just like a tree, a lord of the forest,
> Truly, is a man. . . .
> The hairs of his body are the leaves,
> His skin is the outer bark. . . .
> Blood flows out from his skin
> Like sap from the skin of the tree:
> When he is wounded, it flows out of him
> Like sap from a tree that has been struck.
> His flesh is the outer wood;
> The fibres, so strong, his sinews;
> His bones the hard wood within;
> His marrow made in the likeness of pith.

7. Jochen Zeitz (former chairman and CEO, Puma), interview by author, March 16, 2012.
8. Ibid.
9. Ibid.
10. Ibid.
11. Ibid.
12. Ibid.
13. In Fry and Kriger's model of being-centered leadership, Being-centered leadership is at the highest level and *is defined as leadership based on a business leader's sense of Being or Oneness.* As the authors state, this Oneness is at the core of all major religions and spiritual traditions, a point that I have emphasized while describing the philosophy of the Upanishads.
14. In the most popular and important form of Vedānta, Advaita, the journey is only a metaphorical one from ignorance to knowledge. According to Advaita Vedānta, the lower bird is really an illusion and the higher bird alone is ultimately real. Self-realization occurs when a person realizes that the lower self was false all along and that the Universal Self, or Ātman (which is Being), alone truly exists.

15. Ram Nidumolu, *Organisational Change for Natural Capital Management: Strategy and Implementation*, InnovaStrat, Inc., 2013 http://www.teebforbusiness.org/how/organizational-change-for -natural-capital-management-strategy-and-implementation.html. This study, funded by the TEEB for Business Coalition, collected extensive data on twenty-six pioneering companies that were implementing natural capital management. It focused on leadership as a group effort at the enterprise level, while this book refers to leadership at the individual level.

16. In the Upanishads, *chit* when used with Being typically refers to the higher consciousness associated with the higher reality of *Sat*. Here, in order to be consistent, I use *chit* as it relates to a business leader's consciousness about the larger context of business, which is its higher reality.

17. I use the constructed term *ātmana* because it is easier to pronounce and corresponds to the commonly used term *brāhmaṇa* (knower of Brahman), when compared to other, more technically accurate Sanskrit terms.

Chapter 3

1. Haidt, *The Happiness Hypothesis*, 229.
2. According to Fry and Kriger, Being-centered leadership (Level 1) is the source of inspiration for all the other levels of leadership— spiritual perception at Level 2, moral sensitivity at Level 3, leadership values at Level 4, and traits and behaviors at Level 5. The realization of Being therefore guides a leader's spirituality, morality, values, and traits and behaviors, even while transcending them.

Chapter 4

1. The translation is from Basham, *The Wonder That Was India*, 240–241.
2. See Olivelle, *Upaniṣads*, 69–70; and Juan Mascaro, *The Upanishads* (London: Penguin Books, 1965), 130–31.
3. The other great dependency is on the societal class (*varṇa*) one belongs to.
4. While these four stages were traditionally prescribed for males, I generalize them for everyone.

5. See Herman Daly and Joshua Farley, *Ecological Economics* (Washington, DC: Island Press, 2004), especially chapter 2 ("The Fundamental Vision") for a critique of this and other assumptions of conventional economics.

6. Gurcharan Das, *The Difficulty of Being Good: On the Subtle Art of Dharma* (New York: Oxford University Press, 2009).

7. See Basham, *The Wonder That Was India*, 113, for a discussion.

8. See Damasio, *Self Comes to Mind*, for a discussion.

9. Jim Collins and Jerry Porras, *Built to Last: Successful Habits of Visionary Companies* (New York: HarperBusiness, 2004).

10. This worldview is compatible with that of ecological economists, with Being as the addition.

11. J. M. Cooper, *Pursuits of Wisdom: Six Ways of Life in Ancient Philosophy from Socrates to Plotinus* (Princeton, NJ: Princeton University Press, 2012).

12. See Richard Wilkinson and Kate Pickett, *The Spirit Level* (New York: Bloomsbury Press, 2010), for a fascinating sociological analysis of the extent and impacts of income inequality on society. It nicely complements the economic analysis provided by Stiglitz in *The Price of Inequality*.

13. The value of ecosystem services provided to humanity by nature is estimated at $72 trillion per year, which is comparable to the world's gross national income. However, nearly two-thirds of the world's ecosystems have been degraded because of business as usual. See Joshua Bishop, ed., *The Economics of Ecosystems and Biodiversity in Business and Enterprise* (New York: Earthscan, 2012), for details of how business activity is leading to a loss of natural capital. See the TEEB for Business Coalition website (http://www.teebforbusiness .org) for other reports in this area. Natural capital management is one of the most important emerging disciplines with hundreds of initiatives currently underway.

14. Johan Rockström et al., "Planetary Boundaries: Exploring the Safe Operating Space for Humanity," *Ecology and Society* 14, no. 2 (2009), http://www.ecologyandsociety.org/vol14/iss2/art32/.

15. See Stiglitz, *The Price of Inequality*, and Wilkinson and Pickett, *The Spirit Level*, for details on the growing human and social problems

caused by the increased disparity in income and wealth *within* societies.

16. For a fascinating discussion of how the era of material growth in advanced economies may well be over after three revolutions since 1750, see Robert J. Gordon, "Is US Economic Growth Over? Faltering Innovation Confronts the Six Headwinds," CEPR Policy Insight No. 63, Center for Economic Policy Research, 2012, http://www.cepr.org/pubs/PolicyInsights/CEPR_Policy_Insight_063.asp, and summarized in Robert J. Gordon, "Is US Economic Growth Over? Faltering Innovation Confronts the Six," Vox, September 11, 2012, http://www.voxeu.org/article/us-economic-growth-over.

Chapter 5

1. See Olivelle, *Upaniṣads*, 58–68; and Mascaro, *The Upanishads*, 133–42.
2. For example, see Juan Mascaro, "The Supreme Teaching," in *The Upanishads*, 133–143. Also, see Troy Wilson Organ, *The Hindu Quest for the Perfection of Man* (Athens, OH: Ohio University Press, 1970), 149 (especially Paul Deussen's comments on its uniqueness in the world's literature).
3. The text does not make clear why the sage intended to keep this wisdom a secret. Perhaps it was to build suspense in the story or the sage was tired of being questioned by the king on every visit.
4. *Karma* was also used to describe the fundamental law of cause and effect, which could extend beyond one's lifetime.

Chapter 6

1. See the work by the International Integrated Reporting Council (IIRC) (http://www.theiirc.org/) for more information on integrated reporting.
2. Haidt, *The Happiness Hypothesis*.
3. Daniel Gilbert, *Stumbling on Happiness* (New York: Vintage Books, 2006).

Chapter 7

1. Joel Podolny, "The Buck Stops (and Starts) at Business School," *Harvard Business Review*, June 2009.

Chapter 8

1. See Olivelle, *Upaniṣads*, 190–191; and Mascaro, *The Upanishads*, 110–111.

2. This list is extracted from Sisodia, Wolfe, and Sheth, *Firms of Endearment*, 248.

3. "The Best Advice I Ever Got," *Fortune*, November 12, 2012, 120.

4. Lawrence C. Strauss, "From Texas, with LUV," *Barron's*, February 25, 2012, http://online.barrons.com/article/SB50001424052748703754104577237541929663490.html#articleTabs_article%3D1.

5. By "long-term well-being of the universal self," I mean the long-term well-being of the stakeholder's sense of *connection* to Being.

6. John Mackey and Raj Sisodia, *Conscious Capitalism: Liberating the Heroic Spirit of Business* (Boston: Harvard Business Review Press, 2013).

7. A dharma scorecard (or "balance" scorecard) for business leaders can then track their ability to nurture the well-being of each group of stakeholders at every level of collective self.

8. This sense of collective well-being is captured by the Upanishadic phrase *sarva-bhūta-hite ratāḥ* (the well-being of all beings).

9. For example, it is ranked second in the Global 100 most sustainable companies in the world (http://www.global100.org/annual-lists.html).

10. Samantha Pearson, "In Tune with His Feminine Side," *Financial Times*, December 4, 2011. See http://www.ft.com/intl/cms/s/0/4b6fb0e4-1cf1-11e1-a134-00144feabdc0.html#axzz2QCP7EfnJ.

11. Barbara Seale, "Leadership Profile: Alessandro Carlucci, the Personification of Natura," *Direct Selling News*, December 27, 2011, http://directsellingnews.com/index.php/view/leadership_profile_alessandro_carlucci_the_personification_of_natura#.UWdChKtARRc.

12. Ibid.

13. Ibid.

14. Morten T. Hansen, Herminia Ibarra, and Urs Peyer, "The 100 Best-Performing CEOs in the World," *Harvard Business Review*, January–February 2013.

15. The following material about Dr. V, including excerpts from diaries and quotations, is taken from Pavithra Mehta and Suchitra Shenoy, *Infinite Vision: How Aravind Became the World's Greatest Business Case for Compassion* (San Francisco: Berrett-Koehler, 2012), a book about how the Aravind Eye Care System became an exemplary company for combining high purpose and profits.
16. Mehta and Shenoy, *Infinite Vision*, 27.
17. Ibid., 54.
18. Ibid., 141.
19. Ibid., 122.
20. Ibid., 164.
21. Ibid., 36–37.
22. Ibid., 70.
23. Ibid., 231.
24. Ibid., 232.
25. Krishna Chaitanya, *Gandhi's Quest of Being in Becoming* (New Delhi: Gandhi Peace Foundation, 1977), 20.

Chapter 9

1. Olivelle, *Upaniṣads*, 172–73.
2. Adapted from Olivelle, *Upaniṣads*, 171–5.
3. Olivelle, *Upaniṣads*, 175.
4. See Tim Kasser, *The High Price of Materialism* (Cambridge, MA: MIT Press, 2002), for an excellent and detailed discussion of the relationship between materialism and an unhealthy sense of self.
5. See F. Brochet, G. Serafeim, and M. Loumioti, "Short-Termism: Don't Blame Investors," *Harvard Business Review*, June 2012, for a detailed analysis of over seventy thousand earnings conference calls.
6. Alfred Rappaport, *Saving Capitalism from Short-Termism: How to Build Long-Term Value and Take Back Our Financial Future* (New York: McGraw-Hill, 2011).
7. There's now considerable evidence that long-term orientation leads to greater organizational performance. For example, see Andre de Waal, "Characteristics of High Performance Organisations," *Business Management and Strategy* 3, no. 1 (2012), for a recent extensive testing of the factors that relate positively to organizational

performance. Of the five factors (continuous improvement, openness and action orientation, management quality, workforce quality, and long-term orientation) culled from 290 research studies and tested in 1,470 organizations worldwide, the biggest difference between high-performing and other organizations was in long-term orientation.

8. Jim Collins, *Good to Great: Why Some Companies Make the Leap . . . and Others Don't* (New York: HarperBusiness, 2001), 24.

9. See Sisodia, Wolfe, and Sheth, *Firms of Endearment*, 122, and Wayne F. Cascio, "Decency Means More Than 'Always Low Prices': A Comparison of Costco to Wal-Mart's Sam's Club," *Academy of Management Perspectives*, August 2006, http://www.ou.edu/russell/UGcomp/Cascio.pdf for more information.

10. See Spencer Jakab, "Bulking Up on Costco Is Getting Pricey," *Wall Street Journal*, October 9, 2012, http://online.wsj.com/article/SB100 008723963904432949045780467435024380094.html.

11. David Herrera, "Mondragón: A For-Profit Organization That Embodies Catholic Social Thought," *Review of Business* 25, no. 1 (2004): 56–68; and "Historic Background," Mondragon Corporation, accessed April 22, 2013, http://www.mondragon-corporation.com/ENG/Co-operativism/Co-operative-Experience/Historic-Background.aspx. http://bsr.london.edu/lbs-article/641/index.html.

12. "Leading the Way: Ursula Burns," *Business Strategy Review*, January 2012, http://bsr.london.edu/lbs-article/641/index.html.

13. Ibid.

14. Kai Ryssdal, "Xerox CEO Ursula Burns: Full Interview," *Marketplace*, May 18, 2011, http://www.marketplace.org/topics/business/corner-office/xerox-ceo-ursula-burns-full-interview.

15. The material about Chip Conley is taken from his presentation to the Santa Cruz community, organized by the Santa Cruz Chamber of Commerce, on July 23, 2012.

16. Warren Bennis, *On Becoming a Leader* (New York: Basic Books, 2009), 144.

17. James Burke, "J&J CEO Amid Tylenol Scare," *Wall Street Journal*, October 1, 2012, http://online.wsj.com/article/SB10000872396390 444592404578030681224799460.html.

18. "Lars Rebien Sørensen on Balancing the Demands of Shareholders and Stakeholder's" Principal Voices, accessed April 22, 2013, http://www.principalvoices.com/voices/lars-rebien-sorensen-white-paper.html.
19. Ibid.
20. Ibid.

Chapter 10

1. Olivelle, *Upaniṣads*, 130.
2. John Elkington, "Ray Anderson, Sustainable Business Pioneer, Dies Aged 77," *Guardian*, August 9, 2011, http://www.guardian.co.uk /sustainable-business/blog/ray-anderson-dies-interface-john -elkington-tribute.
3. Emily Langer, "Ray Anderson, 'Greenest CEO in America,' Dies at 77," *Washington Post*, August 10, 2011, http://www.washingtonpost .com/local/obituaries/ray-anderson-greenest-ceo-in-america-dies -at-77/2011/08/10/gIQAGoTU7I_story.html.
4. "Ray Anderson: The Business Logic of Sustainability," TED Talks, filmed February 2009, posted May 2009, http://www.ted.com/talks /ray_anderson_on_the_business_logic_of_sustainability.html.
5. http://raycandersonblog.com/.
6. "Dan Hendrix Discusses Ray Anderson's Legacy as the Founder of Interface," interview by Kemp Harr, Floor Daily.net, August 9, 2011, http://www.floordaily.net/UploadedFiles/RadioInterviews /MP3/Dan%20Hendrix%20Discusses%20Ray%20Andersons%20 Legacy%20as%20the%20Founder%20of%20Interface.mp3.
7. "Ray Anderson: The Business Logic of Sustainability."
8. See the following sources for information on Eileen Fisher: Amanda Coen, "Eileen Fisher Extends Commitment to Environmental, Social Responsibility," Ecouterre, February 2, 2012, http://www .ecouterre.com/eileen-fisher-extends-commitment-to-sustainable -fashion-social-responsibility/; Scott Cooney, "Women in Focus Week, Day 2! Meet the Top Women Sustainable CEOs: Eileen Fisher," Inspired Economist, September 4, 2012, http:// inspiredeconomist.com/2012/09/04/meet-the-top-women -sustainable-ceo-eileen-fisher-womens-week/; and Masha Zager,

-sustainable-ceo-eileen-fisher-womens-week/; and Masha Zager, "Apparel Salutes Its 2012 Sustainability All-Stars Award Winners," Apparel, June 4, 2012, http://m.apparel.edgl.com/MagazineDetail Page.aspx?article=44032.

9. Caitlin A. Johnson, "Eileen Fisher's Unique Business Model," *Sunday Morning*, February 11, 2009, http://www.cbsnews.com/8301-3445 _162-2381285.html.

10. See Olivelle, *Upaniṣads*, 232–237; and Mascaro, *The Upanishads*, 55–64.

11. Cassandra, "Real Hard Numbers: Grantham's Story Problem on Economic Growth," Uncommon Scolds, http://uncommonscolds .wordpress.com/category/jeremy-grantham/.

12. Christian Nellemann and Emily Corcoran, eds., *Dead Planet, Living Planet: Biodiversity and Ecosystem Restoration for Sustainable Development* (Arendal, Norway: United Nations Environment Programme/GRID-Arendal, 2010).

13. World Wide Fund for Nature, *Living Planet Report 2012: Biodiversity, Biocapacity and Better Choices* (Gland, Switzerland: WWF, 2012).

14. Incidentally, it is also a story that arrogates truthfulness to a particular class of society, the brāhmans, which is a giveaway for the social class that the composer of the story belonged to.

15. It is interesting that it was the bull that reminded Satyakāma that the herd had reached a thousand. Satyakāma's bravado seems to have exceeded his diligence in keeping track of his herd.

16. The composer of the Upanishad has the sage teach Satyakāma all over again about reality.

17. John Fullerton, conversation with ServiceSpace's Forest Calls group, August 18, 2012, http://www.awakin.org/forest/?pg=guest&cid=47.

18. Ibid.

19. Ibid.

20. Ibid.

21. For example, the incorporation of environmental, social, and governance (ESG) criteria in investment strategies has reached assets under management valued at $10.7 trillion, which is only 7 percent of the total worldwide market, according to Dinah Koehler and Eric Hespenheide, "Finding the Value in Environmental, Social, and Governance Performance," *Deloitte Review*, 12 (2013).

Chapter 11

1. Paul Polman, "The Remedies for Capitalism," McKinsey & Company, accessed April 22, 2013, http://www.mckinsey.com /features/capitalism/paul_polman.
2. Paul Polman, interview by Adi Ignatius, *Harvard Business Review*, June 2012, 112.
3. Jo Confino, "Paul Polman: Challenging the Corporate Status Quo," *Guardian*, April 24, 2012, http://www.guardian.co.uk/sustainable -business/paul-polman-unilever-sustainable-living-plan.
4. Polman, interview.
5. Polman, "The Remedies for Capitalism."
6. Ibid.
7. Confino, "Paul Polman."
8. Paul Sonne, "Unilever Plows Ahead on Sales Goal," *Wall Street Journal*, January 23, 2013, http://online.wsj.com/article/SB10001424 127887323539804578259022762448496.html.
9. Zeitz, interview.
10. Ibid.
11. Deloitte Innovation BV, *Towards Zero Impact Growth: Strategies of Leading Companies in 10 Industries* (Rotterdam: Deloitte, 2012).
12. Ram Nidumolu, Kevin Kramer, and Jochen Zeitz, "Connecting Heart to Head," *Stanford Social Innovation Review*, November 2011.
13. Robert Eccles, Kathleen Perkins, and George Serafeim, "How to Become a Sustainable Company," *MIT Sloan Management Review* 53, no. 4 (Summer 2012).
14. Mary Jo Hatch and Majken Schultz, eds., *Organizational Identity: A Reader* (Oxford: Oxford University Press, 2004).
15. Another prominent leader-sage from corporate India is Narayana Murthy, the cofounder and former CEO of Infosys. He is a leader-sage because of his great integrity, simplicity, and business success. The heads of the Tata Group of companies in India, such as Jamshedji Tata, J. R. D. Tata, and Ratan Tata, are also exemplary leader-sages. For other examples of wise leaders, see Prasad Kaipa and Navi Radjou's excellent book on wise leadership, *From Smart to Wise: Acting and Leading with Wisdom* (San Francisco: Jossey-Bass, 2013).

16. Azim Premji, "Hard Choices: Wipro's Azim Premji," *Bloomberg-Businessweek Magazine*, September 15, 2010, http://www.business week.com/stories/2010-09-15/hard-choices-wipros-azim-premji.

17. For example, in 2012, *Newsweek* ranked Wipro as number two in its Global 500 Green companies, Greenpeace ranked it as number one among all electronics companies, the Dow Jones Sustainability Index (DJSI) ranked it as number one in the computer services and Internet sector, the Carbon Disclosure Project ranked it as the most sustainable of all Indian companies, and Ethisphere listed it as one of the world's most ethical companies.

18. Azim Premji, "8 Steps to Excellence," Rediff.com, January 17, 2005, http://www.rediff.com/money/2005/jan/17spec.htm.

19. Shehla Raza Hasam, "Great Leaders Do Not Play Games, Says Premji," domain-b, August 1, 2012, http://www.domain-b.com /companies/companies_w/wipro/20020801_games.htm.

20. Naazneen Karmali, "Azim Premji Donates $2.3 Billion after Signing Giving Pledge," *Forbes*, February 23, 2013, http://www.forbes.com /sites/naazneenkarmali/2013/02/23/azim-premji-donates-2-3 -billion-after-signing-giving-pledge/.

21. Premji said in an interview, "If my father had not died, I probably would have stayed in the U.S. and completed a master's degree. Then I would have liked to work for an organization like the World Bank for a few years before coming back. But I have no regrets. It took me a long time, but I finished." Premji, "Hard Choices."

22. See Olivelle, *Upaniṣads*, 128–29.

23. In the text, Raikva is persuaded by the sight of Jānaśruti's daughter. He lifts up her face and says merrily, "With just this face I would have been persuaded." To be honest, I don't know what to make of this, except to think that it was a poor and even sexist attempt at humor by the composer.

24. Stiglitz, *The Price of Inequality*, 32.

25. To Jānaśruti's credit, there was at least philanthropy in his way of gathering merit.

26. See Stiglitz, *The Price of Inequality*, for a discussion of why many financial innovations have been of the rent-seeking variety.

27. Berkshire-Hathaway, Inc., *2012 Annual Report* (Omaha: Berkshire Hathaway, 2013), 2, http://www.berkshirehathaway.com/2012ar /2012a.pdf.
28. Rappaport, *Saving Capitalism from Short-Termism*.
29. Berkshire Hathaway, Inc., *2012 Annual Report*.
30. Ibid.

Conclusion

1. See Organ, *The Hindu Quest for the Perfection of Man*, for an excellent discussion of what freedom (*moksha*) meant in ancient Indian philosophy.

GLOSSARY OF SANSKRIT TERMS

ānanda	Joy or bliss.
āśramas	The four stages of life associated with a human being.
Ātman	The universal self within us that is also Being.
ātmana	A Being-centered leader (a constructed term).
Bhagavad Gītā	A sacred ancient Indian text on the ways to realize Being.
Brahman	Being or reality.
chit	Consciousness.
dharma	Balance, duty, righteousness, eternal law.
Garuda Purāṇa	An ancient Indian text that describes funeral rites.
karma	Work, ritual, law of cause and effect.
moksha	Freedom or liberation associated with realizing Being.
pindas	Food offerings to ancestors during the funeral rituals.
purusha	Spirit, person.
Rig Veda	The oldest and most sacred text of the Veda, dating to 1500-1200 BCE.
Ṛta	Universal order.
Sanskrit	The sacred language of ancient India.
sat	Reality, truth.
sukha	Happiness.
Upanishads	The most important philosophical texts of ancient India.
Vedānta	The end or essence of the Veda.
Veda	The sacred texts of ancient India.

ACKNOWLEDGMENTS

This book exists because of the many people who contributed generously to shaping it over the past years. I am especially grateful to the following, while asking for forgiveness from those unmentioned:

My colleagues who gave me feedback on the book, especially Larry Dressler (by introducing me to Berrett-Koehler, you set this whole thing in motion!), Ulf Wolf, Maren Showkeir, Richard Landry, Richard Callaway, Prasad Kaipa, Jochen Zeitz, John Baker, Kevin Kramer, Chris Laszlo, Carrie Freeman, Jim March, John Ehrenfeld, Jib Ellison, Pavi Mehta, M. R. Rangaswami, Sudip Nandy, Mohan Sodhi, Paul Hawken, Shiv Shivakumar, and many others.

Chip Conley, for readily agreeing to write the foreword for this book (you are an inspiration for Being-centered leaders).

The informal reviewers of this book, especially Danny Chalfen (your encouragement and gentle support have been invaluable), Tim Willcutts (thank you especially for your help with the case studies), Rhiannon Corby, Lauren Schiff, Tre Reinhart, Alysse Guitar, Michelle Magdalena, and many others.

My Stanford creative writing class, especially my instructor, Justin St. Germain, and my classmates who gave feedback on my writing.

My colleagues at the Kozmetsky Global Collaboratory, Stanford University, especially Dr. Syed Shariq, Bhavna Hariharan, Neeraj Sonalkar, Colleen Saxen, Jennifer Keller, Tea Lempiälä, and others (I have benefited immeasurably from our collaboration in creating shareable prosperity).

My friends in my cohousing community, especially Mark Nicolson, Tycho Speaker, Catherine Forest, Steven Mentor, Jennifer Hastings, Kristina Muten, Erica Berg, Adriana Chmiel, and many others who were keen supporters of this book.

My colleagues at Gandiva who were with me through some very difficult times that helped shape this book.

The students of my class on Spirit-Centered Leadership at Sofia University, Palo Alto, who tested some early concepts of this book.

My grandfather Prakasa Rao *garu*, from whom I gained my love of reading; Professor S. K. Chakraborty, who first taught me about management and ancient Indian philosophy; C. K. Prahalad, who encouraged me to write this book; Juan Mascaro for his sublime translation of the Upanishads that first inspired me; and Patrick Olivelle, Sarvepalli Radhakrishnan, Valerie Roebuck, the Ramakrishna Mission, Sri Aurobindo, A. L. Basham, and Troy Organ for their wonderful translations of the Upanishads and other books on the philosophy of ancient India. The Upanishadic stories retold in this book are based mainly on the Olivelle and Mascaro translations.

My family friends, especially Dr. V. R. Venugopal, Jaya Venugopal, Buddy Venugopal, Dr. Ramesh Sinha, Carol and Alan Saltzman, Prathap Sunder, Raju, and others for their encouragement throughout the writing of this book.

My MBA classmates who gave me feedback on this book, especially Derek Nazareth, Atul Rai, Ajay Jain, Jayaram Marthy, T. S. Giridharan, Rao Unnava, Pat Varanasi, and many others.

The *trimurthis* who made this book possible: my editor, Neal Maillet, for his grace, wisdom, guidance, and encouragement throughout this journey (you were the Vishnu who nurtured this book); my managing editor, Jeevan Sivasubramaniam, for seeing this book in me even before I was aware of it (you were the Brahma who initiated this book); and Nic Albert for his invaluable assistance in editing (you were the Shiva who destroyed the unnecessary).

Steve Piersanti and other friends at Berrett-Koehler and their partners who were involved with this book: you lead by example in your mission to create a world that works for all.

Dwarkoji for his inspiring life of service, Dinesh Mehtaji for his selfless efforts to teach me music, and Dr. Saraswati Mohan for her persistent efforts to teach me Sanskrit.

My two dear teachers who have inspired me with their example in the past decade and during the writing of this book: Yogacharya Ellen Grace O'Brian for her love and friendship, unending encouragement, and profound wisdom and Dr. Syed Shariq for his gentleness, enthusiasm, and heartfelt guidance. I have been blessed with knowing you both.

My children, Asha and Ravi (you are the hope of my life), and other members of my birth and extended family: Nanagaru, Amma, Saku, Annu, Ram Babai, Hari, and Keshav (you are the core of my family identity).

Rajesh Krishnan for his selfless help over all these years (you have been my good friend throughout this long journey).

My wife, Kathy—you are the bedrock, companion, and love of my life. I owe all this to you.

The sages and practitioners of the Upanishads who are great examples of lives inspired by Being (*ātmashakti*).

In the end, even if all else is lost, the Ātman that is Being remains.

INDEX

ABOUT THE AUTHOR

Ram Nidumolu is a business consultant, entrepreneur, business scholar, and lifelong student of philosophy. He is the founder and CEO of InnovaStrat, which provides consulting and advisory services to help executives at Fortune 500 companies develop a corporate vision and strategy for sustainable business. He has helped global companies such as FedEx, Alcoa, Intuit, Puma, and others create a compelling strategy around sustainable business, innovation, and technology. His monthly briefings on sustainable business trends are read by hundreds of executives at more than eighty Global 500 corporations.

Ram was the lead author of a celebrated *Harvard Business Review* article "Why Sustainability Is Now the Key Driver of Innovation," which accelerated the field of sustainable innovation. He has also written for *Stanford Social Innovation Review* and other publications.

Ram is recognized globally for his executive insights, practices, and thought leadership in the areas of sustainable business strategy, sustainable innovation, natural capital management, and sustainable business growth. He speaks frequently to business audiences on the future of business leadership, strategy, and innovation.

He was previously a high-tech entrepreneur in Silicon Valley and on the business school faculty at Santa Clara University and the University of Arizona.

Ram is currently also an affiliated scholar at the Kozmetsky Global Collaboratory, Stanford University. He received his doctorate in management at the UCLA Anderson School of Management.

This book synthesizes three fields he has thought deeply about and practiced over the past thirty years: sustainable business, entrepreneurship, and the wisdom traditions.

Ram lives in a cohousing community in Santa Cruz, California, with his family and a domesticated Indian street cat.

Berrett–Koehler
Publishers

A community dedicated to creating
a world that works for all

Dear Reader,

Thank you for picking up this book and joining our worldwide community of Berrett-Koehler readers. We share ideas that bring positive change into people's lives, organizations, and society.

To welcome you, we'd like to offer you a free ebook. You can pick from among twelve of our bestselling books by entering the promotional code **BKP92E** here: http://www.bkconnection.com/welcome.

When you claim your free ebook, we'll also send you a copy of our e-newsletter, the *BK Communiqué*. Although you're free to unsubscribe, there are many benefits to sticking around. In every issue of our newsletter you'll find

- A free ebook
- Tips from famous authors
- Discounts on spotlight titles
- Hilarious insider publishing news
- A chance to win a prize for answering a riddle

Best of all, our readers tell us, "Your newsletter is the only one I actually read." So claim your gift today, and please stay in touch!

Sincerely,

Charlotte Ashlock
Steward of the BK Website

Questions? Comments? Contact me at bkcommunity@bkpub.com.

MIX
Paper from
responsible sources
FSC
www.fsc.org
FSC® C012752

Certified

B

Corporation
bcorporation.net